Freelancing - In Search Of Halal Income

Nurullah Hussain

Freelancing – In Search Of Halal Income

Copyright © 2024 Nurullah Hussain
All rights reserved.

ISBN : 9798839368965

Author's Note

In the name of Allah, the Most Gracious, the Most Merciful.

All praise belongs to Allah, who created you and me as the best of creations. By His special favor, I have had the opportunity to write this book as a guide to earning through freelancing in a halal way from an Islamic perspective.

Freelancing has become very popular recently. We often see news about people earning dollars while working from home. Social media is full of attractive offers promising thousands of dollars with just a few clicks.

It often seems like freelancers are shown as instant money-makers. Kind of money machine you can say! But is it really true? What is the actual story of freelancing? To address these questions, I started writing this book.

Many people ask me, "Is it really possible to earn through freelancing?" While there are already many books on freelancing in the market, **" Freelancing : In Search Of Halal Income"** stands apart. This book focuses on halal freelancing sectors based on the teachings of the Quran and Hadith. In sha Allah, you will find practical guidance here on how to work in a halal manner while understanding the current state of different freelancing sectors.

Freelancing attracts many people because it gives more freedom than traditional jobs. With freelancing, it's possible to earn much more than a regular job with relatively less effort. Stories of successful freelancers often inspire others to start freelancing. But how much of these stories are true? Is it really possible to earn sustainably through freelancing? This book aims to analyze and answer these questions.

There's plenty of advice on starting freelancing or learning new skills. You can find countless books, YouTube videos, and Facebook resources.But what's often missing is a guide on halal freelancing practices. In most cases, the focus is entirely on income, leaving many unaware of how to earn in a halal way. Sadly, this lack of understanding can lead some to unknowingly engage in haram practices.

In today's society, earning through freelancing often gets applause and we appreciate that. But rarely do people question how ethical or halal the work is. For most, the only focus is income, with no concern about how that income is generated. Some even create marketplace accounts without acquiring the necessary skills, which harms their reputation and that of other freelancers in the country.

Freelancing – In Search Of Halal Income

From an Islamic perspective, providing accurate guidance on halal freelancing is crucial. That's why I decided to write this book. In sha Allah, it will benefit both beginners and experienced freelancers.

Living a life guided by halal and haram principles is essential for every individual. However, haram practices have become so widespread that many no longer bother to differentiate. When it comes to freelancing, some think there are no halal opportunities, while others assume that all their efforts are halal simply because they work hard (Astaghfirullah).

This book is dedicated to those who sincerely wish to avoid haram and earn in a halal way. It provides clear, simple, and practical guidance based on my experience and Islamic principles.

If you have any feedback after reading the book, feel free to email me.

Nurullah Hussain
Author and Founder, Sunnah IT Institute
Email: mdnurullah80@gmail.com
Facebook: **fb.com/mdnurullah80**

Freelancing – In Search Of Halal Income

Book Content

Author's Note 3
My Thoughts on Halal Income 7
My Freelancing Journey 9
Understanding Freelancing And Outsourcing 12
I Want to Be a Freelancer 15
Freelancing Marketplaces 17
What is a Freelancing Portfolio and Why it is Important? 21
Learning Skills for Halal Freelancing 24
Graphic Design 28
Digital Marketing 33
Content Writing and Translation 36
UI & UX Design 41
Web Development 44
Website Flipping 48
App Development 52
Data Processing 55
Virtual Assistant 57
Market Research 60
Search Engine Optimization (SEO) 63
Customer Support 67
Project Management 71
Business Consultant 74
Amazon Kindle / Self Publishing 78
Print on Demand 82
Question and answer 87
How Can I Learn by Watching Video Tutorials? 88
What Kind of Computer Do You Need for Freelancing? 91
Laptop or Desktop: Which One is Better? 94
Can I Freelance Without an NID? 96

Which Skill Should I Learn?... 98
Can I Freelance Without Being Fluent in English?.. 100
Which Job is Easier and Offers Higher Income?.. 102
How to Learn Freelancing from Home?... 103
How to Bid and Secure Jobs Easily?.. 105
How to Receive Payment for Freelancing?... 107
Can I Freelance Using a Mobile Phone?... 108
When Should I Bid to Get a Job on a Marketplace?... 109
Why Can Freelance Marketplace Accounts Get Banned?................................... 111
Is it Halal to Do Survey Work on Foreign Websites?...................................... 115
Will a Freelancer Work Late Nights Forever?.. 117
How Can Madrasa Students Freelance?... 119
Can Women Freelance While Maintaining Hijab?.. 122
Can You Freelance While Studying?... 124
Final Words.. 126

My Thoughts on Halal Income

In today's world, online platforms are becoming more and more popular. People are spending a significant amount of their time online, either for necessity or leisure. Today, the internet is creating countless opportunities for earning. People are not just spending time online but also finding ways to generate income. However, very few consider whether their work is halal.

Let's ask ourselves:
"Is the income I'm earning 100% halal?"
If not, have I tried to identify the reasons?
Have I ever approached a knowledgeable scholar or a Mufti to explain my work and ask for a ruling on its permissibility?

For many, the answer might be: "I've never thought about it this way."

Islam encourages earning a halal livelihood through honest effort. There is no place for lies, deceit, or fraud in Islam. Whether it's online or offline, our work must not involve deception, falsehood, or immorality. When we follow these principles, all our efforts will be considered acts of worship, in sha Allah.

The income we earn through hard work for ourselves and our families must be halal. Imagine, on the Day of Judgment, the very people for whom you earned through haram means say, "We don't accept the burden of your haram income!"
How will you feel then? How helpless will you be?

Earning halal income is not optional. It is a fundamental responsibility given to us by Allah. You and I cannot avoid this duty. When you start prioritizing your faith over worldly gains, you'll feel an inner peace that no amount of money can buy. But this peace requires that your income be entirely halal.

We often see people around us earning huge amounts of money through illegal means—buying land, building luxurious homes, and accumulating wealth in countless bank accounts. But these riches will hold no value after death. In fact, even before death, many such people face disgrace and ruin. Their wealth fails to protect them. We've all seen such stories in the news.

Think about it—after death, all we'll have is a piece of land barely big enough for our body and a few pieces of white cloth for our burial. Whether rich or poor, our worldly possessions will not matter. What will make the real difference is our deeds. For some, their sins will drag them to hell, while others will be welcomed into paradise due to their righteous deeds.

As social beings, we are deeply influenced by our surroundings. If the people around us are good, the society will improve. This is why it's essential to stay connected with good, righteous individuals who inspire and guide us. But if we choose the wrong company, we risk straying from the right path.

In freelancing, we might see someone earning a lot of money, buying land, building houses, and traveling the world. These things can make us wish to be like them. But do we ever stop to think about how they're earning? What work they're doing? How much effort they're putting in? And most importantly, is their income halal?

To help you identify who is earning in a halal way or trying to do so, I've created a simple checklist.

Strict adherence to modesty (Hijab) when working with female colleagues.
Ensuring that the work, product, or service contains nothing un-Islamic.
Avoiding music and songs in all forms.
Staying away from any interest-based (riba) transactions.
Staying away from haram businesses or activities.
Avoiding false information or deceptive practices.
Working with team members who are committed to their prayers.
Providing opportunities for prayer and other acts of worship during work hours.

In this book, I have discussed in detail:

- The types of work that can be done in a halal way through freelancing.
- How to work in alignment with Islamic values.
- Methods for learning and mastering these skills effectively.

My Freelancing Journey

I was born in a small town called Bakshiganj Upazila, located in the Jamalpur district of Bangladesh. My father, a humble government employee, and my loving family shaped my early life. As the eldest of two siblings, I grew up with big dreams but little idea of where life would lead me. Like many children, I was encouraged to follow a traditional path—becoming a doctor or an engineer. I, too, aspired to be an engineer and took my first step by enrolling at a textile vocational institute to study textile engineering.

In 2007, I passed my SSC (Secondary School Certificate) from Bakshiganj Upazila, Jamalpur district, Bangladesh securing first place in my school. Afterward, I enrolled at Tangail Textile Institute for a four-year diploma course in textile engineering. At the beginning of my college life in 2007, I did not own a computer, although I had received basic computer training during school. I was always interested in computers, but I didn't have the courage to ask my family for such an expensive item. I remember practicing typing on an old, broken keyboard even though I didn't own a computer.

These days, children often pressure their parents into buying expensive gadgets like mobile phones, cameras, or bikes. Back then, I didn't fully understand the sacrifices a parent makes to see their family happy. During school, when I was learning computers, my teacher often gave me extra time for typing practice and allowed me to type exam questions for other schools. This significantly improved my Bengali (my local language) typing speed, which later proved useful in many areas of my life.

During college, I shared a room with a friend who owned a computer. When he went out to play cricket in the afternoons, he let me use his computer. This allowed me to practice frequently. In my third year of diploma studies, my father finally bought me my first desktop computer (a Dual-Core PC) for $170. After getting my computer, I started learning web programming and practiced photo and video editing on the side. I collected CDs with web development tutorials and began learning how to build websites using Adobe Dreamweaver.

At that time, I didn't know freelancing could be a source of income. I started learning web development out of pure interest, dreaming of creating my own website where I could share my information.

After completing my diploma education degree, I started working at a textile

Freelancing – In Search Of Halal Income

factory (Epyllion Group) in 2011 with a monthly salary of just $60/month. Simultaneously, I enrolled in a B.Sc. program in Textile Engineering in Dhaka, using $200 from my family. Each semester required about $120- $130, which I could not fully cover with my salary. To cover my expenses, I worked two tuition jobs and managed to save $30–$40 each month for my semester fees.

During this period, my days were filled with responsibilities: working shifts at the textile factory, attending classes once a week, and studying for exams. I also squeezed in time to practice web development. Many days, after night shifts, I went directly to the university for classes or exams. I remember saving money by skipping meals, choosing cheaper clothes, and carefully managing every expense to stay within my budget.

Eventually, I created an account on the oDesk marketplace (now Upwork) and started taking on small jobs. Over several months, I earned about $300, which boosted my confidence. In 2013, I quit my job and moved to Dhaka to focus on improving my skills. My uncle supported me during this time, and I stayed at his place in Uttara, Dhaka, Bangladesh.

I decided to take a semester break from my B.Sc. studies to dedicate four months to building my career. During this time, I joined online communities on Facebook and YouTube for support and guidance. I also connected with Rasel Ahmed from RR Foundation, whose tutorials were very helpful. Inspired by this, I started a YouTube channel called "Tutorial Tube," which I later renamed "Freelancing Care" on September 21, 2013. I began uploading short tutorials on web development. Today, the channel has over 430k subscribers.

After completing my B.Sc. in Textile Engineering, I didn't return to a regular job. Gradually, I began receiving more work on various platforms, including Fiverr, Upwork, Freelancer, and PeoplePerHour. Having a good command of English helped me learn quickly and communicate effectively with clients. The early days of my freelancing career demanded a lot of effort and dedication.

By 2015, my freelancing career had gained momentum. I received the BASIS (Bangladesh Association of Software and Information Services) Outsourcing Award as the best freelancer from Jamalpur district. This recognition fueled my passion further, and in 2017, I formed a small team to expand my services. Later, I shifted my focus to creating and selling themes, templates, and plugins through my own website. In 2020, I was honored again with the BASIS Outsourcing Award for my contributions to the freelancing industry.

Today, I run a business that provides IT services globally, selling themes, templates, and plugins. I also run a local IT training center called Sunnah IT Institute (sunnahit.com), where many students learn the skills needed for earning halal income online.

Freelancing – In Search Of Halal Income

Looking back, I see that the challenges I faced were stepping stones to success. Every hardship, from skipping meals to late-night study sessions, taught me resilience, patience, and gratitude.

To anyone who wants to start freelancing, I want to say:

"Your current circumstances do not determine your future. Dream big, work hard, and never lose hope."

Start small and stay consistent. Focus on improving your skills instead of comparing yourself to others. Remember, success doesn't happen overnight—it takes patience and effort.

Trust in Allah's plan, and don't let fear of failure stop you. Work sincerely and honestly, and Allah will guide you and provide what is best for you. Keep moving forward, and celebrate even the small achievements along the way.

Alhamdulillah, I am thankful for the blessings Allah has given me. Please keep me in your prayers, and I hope my story inspires you to believe in yourself and follow your dreams.

Understanding Freelancing And Outsourcing

The word "freelancing" means independent work or a free profession, something most of us are already familiar with. Freelancing allows you to work independently, based on your skills and preferences.

In traditional jobs, you usually have to follow strict routines: showing up at the office at 8 or 9 in the morning, working five or six days a week, and facing your boss's reprimands if something goes wrong. There's little room for flexibility or creativity, and your salary is fixed regardless of your performance.

Freelancing is different. You're not tied to one employer. If you don't like working with a client, you can move on to another. You can choose who to work with, set your own hours, and work from home. This freedom lets you spend more time with your family and take breaks whenever you need to, without asking for permission.

Freelancing also gives you the freedom to dedicate time to worship. You can leave work to perform Itikaf or Umrah without needing anyone's approval.

From these benefits, it's clear that freelancing is an independent way of working, free from the restrictions of a fixed employer.

Many people think freelancing means sitting at a computer all day. But freelancing isn't limited to the online world—it can be done offline too. For example, if you're good at writing stories, articles, or poems, you can work as a freelance writer. Even writing by hand and sending your work to a newspaper is considered freelancing. However, this book focuses only on online freelancing from an Islamic perspective.

Here's an example: Suppose you are skilled at designing logos. I need a logo for my business, so I hire you and pay you for your work. This is the model of freelancing. Alternatively, I could have hired an in-house graphic designer on a monthly salary. While this approach works for companies with consistent design needs, it comes with certain challenges. Employing an in-house designer requires a long-term commitment, regardless of the workload. For instance, even during times when there's little or no design work, I would still be obligated to pay their salary, along with other potential benefits like office space, equipment, and health insurance.

Freelancing – In Search Of Halal Income

Freelancing provides flexibility to both the client and the service provider. As a client, I may hire excellent freelancers as needed, allowing me to avoid long-term commitments and unnecessary overhead costs. It allows the freelancer to work with many clients, choose tasks of interest, and choose their own timetable.

Freelancing creates a win-win situation. Businesses can access talented people from around the world without the limits of traditional hiring, while freelancers can work independently, explore different opportunities, and earn based on their skills and hard work.

This model is especially appealing in today's fast-paced digital world, where businesses often require on-demand services without the burden of maintaining a full-time team. It also allows freelancers to build their careers, grow their expertise, and create value for clients across industries—all while enjoying the flexibility of working on their own terms.

Freelancing is possible in many fields, and your income depends on your skills. In a traditional job, your salary is fixed and may not increase as per your expectations. However, as a freelancer, your income is not limited. Some months, you might earn several times more than you expected. There's no need to wait for a raise—it depends entirely on your workload and skills.

Freelancing is not something you "learn" as a skill itself. First, you need to learn specific work skills, such as graphic design, web development, or writing. Then, you apply those skills to freelancing. Saying, "I want to learn freelancing," is like saying, "I want to learn a job." Instead, focus on learning a skill that will allow you to freelance.

Freelancing vs. Outsourcing

Many people confuse freelancing with outsourcing, but they are entirely different concepts. Let me clarify:

- **Freelancing**: When you work independently and complete tasks for someone else, you are freelancing.
- **Outsourcing**: When a company hires someone external (like a freelancer) to complete specific tasks instead of hiring a full-time employee, it's outsourcing.

For example, if I ask you to design a logo for my company, you are freelancing, and I am outsourcing the task.

Why Companies Outsource?

It's natural to wonder why companies choose outsourcing when they can hire their own in-house designers, developers, marketers, writers, or SEO experts. Let's break it down.

Hiring a permanent employee involves several steps and expenses. A company needs to: Set up an office, Purchase equipment, such as computers, Allocate dedicated desks and resources.

Even after all this, if there isn't enough work, the employee will remain idle, but their monthly salary still needs to be paid.

Outsourcing solves this problem. By hiring freelancers for specific tasks, companies save on these fixed costs. They don't have to worry about setting up offices, maintaining equipment, or paying salaries when there's no work.

Moreover, outsourcing allows tasks to be completed faster since freelancers are often highly skilled in their specific areas of work. This is why many companies prefer outsourcing. It helps them reduce costs while maintaining efficiency.

By outsourcing tasks through marketplaces like Upwork or Fiverr, companies can also access a global pool of talent and ensure work is completed quickly and effectively. In this way, companies can achieve more in less time without the long-term commitment of hiring permanent employees.

Companies often outsource through marketplaces like Upwork or Fiverr, which provide payment protection for freelancers. Additionally, companies may hire freelancers directly through platforms like **Facebook** or **LinkedIn**.

Important Notes
Freelancing is not something you learn; you learn a skill to freelance.
Freelancing and outsourcing are not the same.
Freelancers: People who do the work.
Outsourcers: People or companies who hire freelancers to do the work.

In the next, I'll discuss freelancing marketplaces and how they work. Stay tuned!

I Want to Be a Freelancer

A true freelancer is someone actively involved in freelance work. Online freelancers work from home, while offline freelancers work outside on various projects. However, there's another type of so-called freelancer often seen on social media—people who add "freelancer" to their profiles despite having little to no work history on marketplaces. After finishing one or two small projects, they go around showing off the freelancer title.

Unfortunately, many of us are inspired by such people to open marketplace accounts without even considering the halal-haram aspects. We don't take the time to learn a skill, let alone assess whether the work is permissible. Our focus is solely on earning thousands of dollars.

But is it truly that easy to earn dollars in a halal way? Just opening an account on a marketplace won't make clients flood your account with money. Marketplaces are global platforms where freelancers from all over the world compete for the same job. Freelancers from Bangladesh, India, Pakistan, the Philippines, Indonesia, the USA, and many other countries compete for the same projects.

Clients won't hand over projects based on appearances or social media interactions. They choose the most experienced and skilled candidate. Giving a "love" reaction to a Facebook post by some self-proclaimed freelancer won't land you a job.

To become a true freelancer, your primary focus must be on learning skills. Once you have mastered a skill, only then should you consider creating a marketplace account and applying for jobs.

This book doesn't merely guide you on how to create a marketplace account or list the types of jobs available. Instead, it emphasizes building the necessary skills and sustaining your freelancing career. A skilled freelancer can figure out how to create accounts and secure jobs independently.

The Real Freelancers

For example, in the screenshot bellow *(taken from a public Upwork profile as per Upwork's privacy policy)*, a Bangladeshi freelancer named Atikur Rahman earned over $100,000 by completing 790 projects related to fillable PDF forms and editing. He charges $15 per hour for his work.

Atiqnur R. Bangladesh
Fillable PDF Form, PDF Edit, JavaScript, Acrobat PRO & Conditional Cal
$15/hr   98% Job Success $100K+ earned

If you want to find such genuine freelancers earning significant amounts, skip social media and head to marketplaces like Upwork or Fiverr. On these platforms, you can explore freelancer profiles, check the types of work they do, and see client feedback. Genuine freelancers are often less active on social media due to their busy schedules.

Beware of Scams

Unfortunately, many young people are misled by flashy social media ads and fake freelancers offering overpriced courses. They are lured by promises of quick, massive earnings, only to end up disappointed.

Instead of falling for these traps, take your time to learn a professional skill first. Once you've mastered a skill, you can think about freelancing. Remember, freelancing is not something you "learn." You learn a skill first, such as graphic design, digital marketing, writing, or app development, and then apply that skill to freelance work.

Choosing the Right Freelancing Path

There are countless freelancing categories, such as: Graphic Design, Digital Marketing, Writing and Translation, UI/UX Design, Web Development, App Development, Virtual Assistance, Search Engine Optimization (SEO), Customer Support, Project Management, Business Consulting, Legal Consulting, Amazon Kindle Publishing etc.

Before choosing a category, ensure that it offers sufficient opportunities for halal work. Research the experiences of others in the field and learn how they distinguish between halal and haram practices.

Freelancing isn't just about making money; it's about ensuring that your work aligns with Islamic principles. By choosing the right path and dedicating yourself to learning, you can build a successful and halal freelancing career.

Freelancing Marketplaces

Some of you reading this book may not be familiar with the term "marketplace." Simply put, a marketplace is a platform where freelancers compete for work, and companies or clients post jobs to hire freelancers of their choice. It functions similarly to the well-known website indeed.com.

On indeed.com, you can browse job posts by category and apply for positions. Companies post jobs to recruit employees, and they can view your profile, which includes your photo, academic qualifications, professional experience, and other personal details.

Freelancing marketplaces operate in the same way but on a global scale. Freelancers create accounts and build profiles showcasing their skills. Before hiring, clients review these profiles to find the best fit for their projects.

There's a common saying that you can't get a job without the help of connections like uncles or acquaintances. Often, those without such connections end up going to interviews but fail to land the job. However, things are improving, especially in the private sector, where skills are being prioritized over academic qualifications, particularly in the IT field.

Freelancing marketplaces make things even easier. Here, you don't need connections to succeed. You just need to learn a skill, create an account, build a professional profile, and regularly apply for jobs. Eventually, you'll land your first project.

The best part? You don't need to spend money to join these marketplaces. All it takes is patience. Some people get their first job within a week, while others may take a month or even several months.

But patience and persistence are crucial. If you give up after failing to get work initially, you won't succeed in freelancing marketplaces. Stick with it, keep improving your skills, and opportunities will come your way.

Popular Freelancing Marketplaces

Below are some popular freelancing marketplaces along with their details:

Name	Website Link	Founded	Country
Upwork	upwork.com	2015	USA
Fiverr	fiverr.com	2010	Israel
Freelancer	freelancer.com	2009	Australia
Guru	guru.com	1998	USA
SEOClerks	seoclerks.com	2011	USA
Legiit	legiit.com	2018	USA
PeoplePerHour	pph.me	2007	UK
99designs	99designs.com	2007	Australia

Among these, Fiverr is particularly popular among freelancers worldwide due to its ease of use and quicker job opportunities. Many beginners start their freelancing journey on Fiverr and manage to land work within a short time.

Key Tips for Marketplaces

Skill First: You must have a skill before creating a marketplace account. Without proper skills, it will be challenging to sustain your profile.

Free to Join: Most freelancing marketplaces are free to join, but some offer paid membership plans for additional benefits. Be cautious of fraudulent sites that ask for money to create accounts.

Use Your Own ID: Always create accounts using your own National ID (NID) and in your own name. Avoid using family members' accounts, as it can lead to issues later.

Types of Work in Marketplaces:

- **Hourly Basis**: Clients pay you based on the hours worked.
- **Project-Based**: Fixed-price contracts for specific projects.
- **Gig Services**: Selling pre-defined services or gigs at a set price.

By understanding how these marketplaces operate, you can set up your freelancing career in a structured and halal manner.

Hourly Work

In hourly work, freelancers are paid based on the number of hours they work.

A common question is how the client monitors the hours worked. Marketplaces that support hourly work usually have their own software. Freelancers turn on this software while working, allowing clients to monitor their work directly.

The software takes periodic screenshots of the freelancer's computer screen, which are logged and made accessible to the client. Along with screenshots, the software records activity levels, such as the number of clicks and key presses, providing an activity score. This ensures that payment is only made for actual work, not just for keeping the software running.

While working hourly, it's essential to avoid wasting time, as the client is paying for every second. For instance, if you're hired at $15 per hour but take significantly longer than expected due to negligence, the client may suffer financial loss. Conversely, if you complete the work faster, the client saves money and may prefer to work with you again. Therefore, honesty and diligence are crucial qualities for freelancers.

Contract-Based (Fixed-Rate) Work

In contract-based work, freelancers and clients agree on a fixed budget for completing a project. Clients provide detailed job descriptions on marketplaces, and freelancers from around the world submit proposal letters to apply for the job.

It's common for clients to request samples before awarding a project. This helps them evaluate whether the freelancer is suitable for the job and has prior experience with similar tasks. However, some unethical individuals may attempt to exploit freelancers by asking for free work under the guise of a "test project." While such cases are rare, it's important to carefully review the client's profile before accepting work.

Check whether the client has previously worked on the marketplace, the feedback they've received from other freelancers, and the total amount they've paid through the platform. This due diligence minimizes the risk of scams. As freelancers striving to earn in a halal way, we must avoid deceiving others and ensure that we're not deceived ourselves.

Selling Services or Gigs (Fixed Price)

When selling services or gigs, freelancers list their offerings with a description and a set price. For example, you might list, "I will design a logo for $50." Clients can browse your service and purchase it if they're interested.

To create a strong profile for selling gigs, include a well-curated portfolio and accurate information about yourself. Never copy details from other freelancers' profiles. Present yourself uniquely to stand out, so clients develop a positive impression when they view your profile.

Remote Jobs: A Valuable Alternative

Aside from freelancing marketplaces, remote jobs are another excellent opportunity for earning. Remote jobs often involve working for a single company on a long-term basis while enjoying the flexibility of working from home.

Popular platforms for remote job listings include:

- We Work Remotely (weworkremotely.com)
- Remote OK (remoteok.io)
- FlexJobs (flexjobs.com)

Remote jobs are particularly appealing for those seeking stability, as they typically come with consistent pay and clearly defined roles. Unlike freelancing, where you juggle multiple clients, remote jobs allow you to focus on a single employer. However, the application process is often more competitive and requires a well-crafted resume tailored to remote roles.

How to create a standout profile and secure work quickly?

Many people ask for tips on how to create a good profile and get work quickly. To create a strong profile, include a well-organized portfolio, provide accurate information about yourself, and ensure your profile is error-free. Never copy information from other freelancers' profiles to use in yours. Always strive to present yourself uniquely so that clients get a positive impression as soon as they view your profile.

To get work quickly, carefully read the job description before placing a bid. Avoid sending copy-paste cover letters to clients. Instead, write a customized cover letter tailored to the specific job, incorporating the details mentioned in the job post. This shows the client that you've thoroughly read their job description before bidding. Otherwise, they may consider your bid as spam.

What is a Freelancing Portfolio and Why it is Important?

A portfolio is a curated collection of samples or examples that demonstrate the quality and scope of the work you do or the services you provide, all presented on a single platform. It serves as a professional showcase that allows potential clients or employers to understand your skills, experience, and creativity at a glance. Naturally, the content and structure of a portfolio will vary based on the profession or field it represents.

For instance, the portfolio of a web developer will differ significantly from that of a graphic designer, and similarly, an article writer's portfolio will look completely different from an SEO expert's portfolio. Each profession involves distinct skills and deliverables, so the portfolio should be tailored to reflect the unique nature of the work.

Here are some examples to illustrate this:

- **Web Developer**: A web developer demonstrates their expertise by showcasing the websites they have built. Their portfolio may include live links to websites, descriptions of the functionality and features they developed, and details about the technologies they used (e.g., HTML, CSS, JavaScript, React, or WordPress). This allows clients to explore their work and assess their capabilities in creating responsive, user-friendly, and visually appealing websites.

- **Article Writer**: An article writer showcases their skills through samples of different types of articles, such as blog posts, research-based articles, how-to guides, or opinion pieces. Their portfolio might also include links to articles published online, excerpts from longer works, and testimonials from satisfied clients. This provides potential clients with an understanding of the writer's tone, style, and expertise in covering various topics.

- **Graphic Designer**: A graphic designer's portfolio is a visual representation of their creativity and technical skills. It might include samples of logos, business cards, brochures, posters, illustrations, social media graphics, and other design work. The portfolio could also highlight projects they've completed for clients, showcasing their ability to meet diverse design needs and follow brand guidelines.

- **SEO Expert**: An SEO expert's portfolio focuses on demonstrating their ability to improve website rankings and traffic. It may include case studies, screenshots of analytics showing results, examples of keyword research, on-page optimizations, and details about strategies they implemented for successful campaigns.

- **Digital Marketer**: A digital marketer's portfolio emphasizes their ability to drive campaigns and achieve measurable results. It might include social media campaign performance metrics (e.g., engagement, reach, and conversion rates), Google Analytics reports, examples of ad creatives, content calendars, and strategies for improving brand visibility. Highlighting specific achievements, such as doubling a client's website traffic or reducing ad spend while increasing conversions, can make the portfolio stand out.

In this way, each profession requires a portfolio that aligns with the specific nature of its services, tailored to highlight the most relevant and impactful aspects of the individual's work.

Why Do You Need a Portfolio?

Imagine you are hiring a driver. The first things you would consider are whether they have previous driving experience, their accident history, and if they have a valid driving license. The driver's past work demonstrates their skills, the license confirms their qualifications, and their previous employers serve as their portfolio.

Similarly, when you bid for freelance work, the client or buyer might ask to see samples of your previous work. For example, if you're a web developer, the client might request links to your top three websites. This is where a portfolio becomes essential. A portfolio website showcases your work beautifully.

How to Build and Present a Portfolio

There are several ways to create a portfolio:

Portfolio Platforms: Websites like Behance, Adobe Portfolio, Wix, Weebly, and GitHub allow you to build an online portfolio for free or at minimal cost. These platforms are particularly popular among designers, developers, and other creatives.

Freelance Marketplaces: Many marketplaces, such as Upwork or Fiverr, allow freelancers to include their past work directly in their profiles. If your marketplace profile has a strong work history, it can serve as your portfolio link.

Personal Website: If you want full control over your portfolio, consider creating your own website. A personal website allows you to showcase your work and brand in a highly customized way. However, it may involve additional costs for a domain, hosting, and possibly hiring a developer if you're not confident in building the site yourself.

Sharing Links and Following Marketplace Policies

When sharing portfolio links on freelancing platforms, be mindful of their policies. For example:

- Avoid sharing links to other marketplaces (e.g., Fiverr links on Upwork), as this may be interpreted as encouraging clients to work outside the platform.
- If you share your personal portfolio website, ensure it doesn't include direct contact information like your phone number or email. Marketplaces may assume you are trying to bypass their commission system, which can lead to account suspension.

By adhering to these policies, you can ensure that your account remains in good standing while effectively sharing your work.

Ethical Practices

Your portfolio must reflect your genuine work and skills. Never use someone else's portfolio as your own, as it is unethical and can damage your reputation. Always present your abilities honestly to build trust with clients.

A strong, truthful portfolio is crucial for showcasing your capabilities and securing freelance work.

Learning Skills for Halal Freelancing

Now that we've discussed freelancing, marketplaces, and portfolios, let's look at how to start freelancing in a halal way.

When we think of freelancing, we often connect it with web design, graphic design, or digital marketing since these topics are commonly talked about. However, freelancing actually spans a wide range of fields. Alhamdulillah, if we follow some basic and common principles, we can freelance in various categories in a halal way.

It's well known that business is halal and even a Sunnah of our beloved Prophet Muhammad ﷺ. However, even a halal business can lead to sin if we cheat, deceive, or lie in the process.

Imagine a tea shop. Running a tea shop is halal; anyone can open one, as business itself is permissible. But what if I install a TV in my shop and constantly play music, vulgar dances, or immoral content? If customers gather to watch these programs while drinking tea and I use this to increase my sales, my tea shop becomes a source of sin. At this point, I'm not earning from selling tea but from promoting immorality.

Similarly, think of a job. If I perform my duties sincerely, respect my working hours, and fulfill my responsibilities, my earnings will be halal. But if I start demanding bribes for signatures, refuse to process files without extra money, or engage in oppression, my halal job turns into a constant source of haram income. Many people unknowingly or intentionally turn halal jobs into haram income sources.

The same applies to freelancing. A good profession can easily involve haram or prohibited actions. Therefore, we must have control over ourselves, maintain fear of Allah in our hearts, and avoid greed. After all, how much money do we need to survive? Our sustenance has already been determined by Allah. If I fail to earn it in a halal way, that failure is entirely mine.

In the Holy Quran, Allah says:

"There is no moving creature on earth whose provision is not guaranteed

Freelancing – In Search Of Halal Income

by Allah." [1]

Allah has clearly stated that He is responsible for the sustenance of all creatures. If we doubt this, it undermines our faith. Hence, my sustenance will surely come to me, but it's my responsibility to seek it in a halal way. The rest is in Allah's hands.

Allah also says:

"No soul knows what it will earn tomorrow, nor does any soul know in which land it will die."[2]

We do not know what we will earn in the future. Everything is preordained. Our job is to strive, and the outcome will align with the decree of Allah.

When pursuing freelancing, I must think about how to earn my sustenance in a halal manner. I must consider whether my work is being conducted appropriately. Before learning a particular skill, I need to investigate how much halal work is available in that field.

No freelancing category can be entirely labeled as halal or haram. To determine this, we must first understand the processes and practices involved in the specific category.

Freelancing offers a wide range of opportunities, and among them, the following categories are notable for halal work:

- Graphics Design
- Digital Marketing
- Writing and Translation
- UI/UX and Web Design
- Web Development
- Website Flipping
- App Development
- Data Processing
- Market Research
- Search Engine Optimization (SEO)
- Customer Care
- Project Management

---

[1] Surah Hud: 6
[2] Surah Luqman: 34

Freelancing – In Search Of Halal Income

- Business Consultant
- Amazon Kindle/Self-Publishing
- Print on Demand
- Virtual Assistant

Other halal categories may also exist beyond this list. However, the mentioned categories are generally easier to approach while ensuring halal practices.

Each of these categories includes numerous subcategories. For instance:

Graphics Design Subcategories: Logo Design, Illustration, Pattern Design, Storyboard, Photoshop Editing, Infographic Design, Web Banners, Email Template Design, Interior Design, T-Shirt Design, Jewelry Design, Flyer Design, Brochure Design, Signage Design, Poster Design, Postcard Design, Invitation Card Design etc.

Web Design Subcategories: WordPress, Website Builders and CMS, E-commerce Websites, Mobile Applications, Desktop Applications, IT Support, Chatbot Development, Cybersecurity, Software Testing etc.

Digital Marketing Subcategories: Social Media Marketing, Social Media Advertising, SEO (Search Engine Optimization), Public Relations, Content Marketing, Email Marketing, SEM (Search Engine Marketing), E-commerce Marketing, Mobile App Marketing etc.

Video and Animation Work: Whiteboard Explainers, Logo Animation, Subtitle Captions, E-commerce Product Videos, Intro/Outro Videos, Product Photography etc.

Avoid projects involving music or inappropriate visuals, such as immodest content.

By focusing on any one of these categories, you can specialize in a particular skill, laying the foundation for a rewarding career in freelancing. Each category offers numerous opportunities to build expertise and start earning a halal income, Insha'Allah.

For example, if you choose Graphic Design, it's better to start by mastering one subcategory rather than trying to learn everything at once. You could focus on Logo Design, developing skills to create visually compelling and memorable logos for brands. Alternatively, you might specialize in Infographic Design, presenting data and information in a visually engaging way. Both areas are in high demand and can help you gain expertise and start offering professional services.

Freelancing – In Search Of Halal Income

As you get better in one subcategory, you can gradually expand to other areas like social media graphics, business card design, or poster creation. This step-by-step approach builds your confidence, sharpens your skills, and helps you create a portfolio that showcases expertise in specific areas, making you more appealing to clients.

Similarly, if you're interested in Web Design, start with WordPress development. Begin by building simple blogs or portfolio websites, and then move on to more complex e-commerce websites using tools like WooCommerce or Shopify. This gradual progression allows you to specialize in high-demand niches while improving your skills.

By focusing on one area first, you can deliver high-quality work that meets client expectations. Specialization helps you stand out in a competitive marketplace. Once established, you can explore related services to expand your offerings and grow your earning potential.

For example, many freelancers begin with logo design and eventually offer full branding packages, including letterheads, business cards, and social media templates. Similarly, web designers often expand into SEO optimization, website maintenance, or custom plugin development once they've built a strong reputation.

The key is to commit to one skill at a time, ensuring that you develop a strong understanding of its tools, techniques, and applications. Once you've mastered the basics, you can build a portfolio that showcases your work, making it easier to attract clients. Whether it's Social Media Marketing, Video Editing, or Cybersecurity, every subcategory holds immense potential if approached with dedication and consistency.

The upcoming chapters will guide you through the steps to acquire these skills, from finding the right learning resources to practical tips for honing your craft. You'll also learn how to apply your knowledge effectively in freelance marketplaces, communicate with clients, and deliver results that align with halal principles. With focus, patience, and reliance on Allah, you can embark on a journey toward financial independence and a fulfilling career, Insha'Allah.

Important Notes
Freelancing offers numerous categories to explore
You can specialize in just one category to start freelancing.
Each category contains multiple subcategories.
No category is inherently halal or haram; it depends on the nature of the work

Graphic Design

Graphic design is an art form where an artist creates visual concepts using computer software to communicate ideas, information, and client requirements. While the definition of graphic design might seem complex, the work itself is delightful. Graphic design can be a great profession to showcase your creativity. Among the various tasks, logo design, business card design, brochure design, and product packaging are relatively easier. You can enhance your skills by starting with these smaller tasks. Don't try to learn everything at once. Start with business card design, which is a common starting point. To learn, search for designs on websites like Google, GraphicRiver, or Freepik. Choose a simple design and try replicating it. For graphic design work, you'll need software like Photoshop, Illustrator, or Figma. Alternatively, you can use Canva or Wepik to create designs easily. Spend some time learning these tools or software.

After learning graphic design, you can earn money in many ways. For instance, if you excel in logo design, you can earn through marketplaces or participate in contests on websites like 99designs. These sites host competitions for logo designs, where one winner is selected and rewarded. Since these contests don't require entry fees, they don't fall under gambling. If the company is halal and doesn't require using images of living beings in the logo, participating is permissible. [3] [4] [5]

To design logos in a halal way, you must avoid haram elements or themes. Be cautious about this. Once, a man sought permission from Ibn Abbas (RA) to draw pictures. He replied, "If you must draw for earning, then draw trees or images that do not depict living beings." [6] This hadith makes it clear that designing non-living things generally poses no issues as long as the work serves no haram purpose.

For instance, if an alcohol company requests a logo design that doesn't involve haram imagery, you should still decline as the intent is haram. Similarly, projects involving interest-based institutions or usury should also be avoided. My advice

---

[3] Ad-Durrul Mukhtar: 9/577
[4] Kefayatul Mufti: 9/225
[5] Sahih Muslim - 2110
[6] Sahih Bukhari - 2225

would be to politely decline such work. You can message the client, saying, "In my religion, alcohol, gambling, and interest are prohibited, so I do not work on such projects. However, if you need help with other business needs, feel free to contact me." Such a message not only declines the work politely but also serves as a form of da'wah. The client, unaware that alcohol, gambling, and interest are prohibited in Islam, might learn something beautiful about Islamic values through you. Many avoid explicit haram work like pornography but engage in interest-based projects, claiming they aren't doing anything wrong. Therefore, it's important to stay vigilant about these subtle matters to ensure your work remains halal.

Similarly, imagine a client wants to design a logo for a restaurant. While their business is halal, the logo includes imagery that contradicts Islamic principles. In such cases, you should avoid taking on the project. Insha'Allah, if you selectively choose your projects with such care, Allah will bless your earnings with barakah and provide you with more than you can imagine.

Another simple area in graphic design is photo retouching and background removal. When working in this category, you must avoid retouching images of women. The same principle applies to background removal. You can work on non-living objects or products without any issues.

For example, if I own a grocery store and want the product photos on my website to have a white background, I might hire you to make those adjustments. Alhamdulillah, there is nothing haram in such work. However, if a client provides a picture of a female model and asks you to remove the background—often done for jewelry or fashion-related e-commerce businesses—you should decline the project. To earn halal income, these considerations must always be taken into account when working on photo retouching or background removal tasks.

Allah says,

"**Do not approach immorality—whether it is apparent or concealed.**"[7]

How to Learn Graphic Design

The internet offers a wealth of resources for learning graphic design, with **YouTube** being one of the most accessible platforms. By simply searching for terms like **"graphic design tutorial"**, you'll find countless videos covering

---

[7] Surah An'am - 151

various topics, from beginner basics to advanced techniques. For instance, if you're interested in learning **logo design**, searching **"logo design tutorial"** will yield numerous helpful resources. These tutorials not only teach technical skills but also help you understand the purpose and impact of design elements.

To learn effectively, it's important to start with the basics. Ask questions like:

- What is a logo?
- Why is it used?
- What makes a logo effective?

By exploring these topics on Google or YouTube, you can build a strong foundational understanding. To access high-quality tutorials by renowned international designers, always try searching in **English**. This will give you a broader perspective on global design standards and techniques.

Diversifying Your Learning Methods

While video tutorials are excellent for learning specific techniques, supplementing them with other resources can greatly enhance your skills. For example:

- **Read design-related blogs**: Websites and blogs written by experienced designers offer valuable insights, tips, and industry updates.
- **Observe and analyze others' work**: Platforms like **GraphicRiver.net** showcase various design elements such as logos, T-shirt designs, brochures, product packaging, vector icons, banners, newsletters, and user interfaces. By studying these, you can learn about current trends, international standards, and effective design principles.

However, observation alone is not enough. To truly improve, you must practice regularly. Apply what you've learned by creating your own designs. Start with simple projects and gradually challenge yourself with more complex tasks.

Overcoming Challenges as a Beginner

When you start designing, it's normal to encounter difficulties. Your first designs might not meet professional standards, or you might struggle with certain tools and techniques. Don't let this discourage you. Instead, treat each challenge as an opportunity to learn.

If you face issues with a specific design aspect, such as using a tool or creating an effect, search for targeted tutorials on YouTube. For example, if you're unsure how to create a gradient effect, search **"how to create gradients in Photoshop"** and follow the step-by-step instructions in the videos. Regular practice will help you master these techniques over time.

Engaging with the Design Community

Joining a community of like-minded individuals is incredibly motivating and helpful for growth. If you're looking for international design communities, here are some popular options:

- Dribbble: Showcase your work, get inspired, and connect with designers globally (dribbble.com).
- Behance: Display your portfolio and interact with designers worldwide (behance.net).
- Designers Talk: Forum-based discussions on trends, tools, and techniques (designerstalk.com).
- Reddit: Subreddits like r/graphic_design and r/web_design for feedback and discussions.
- Graphic Design Forum: Engage in sharing ideas and projects (graphicdesignforum.com).
- Slack Communities: Join Designership or Designer Hangout for collaboration and learning.
- Awwwards: Explore exceptional web design and join discussions (awwwards.com).
- CreativePool: Network with professionals and find design inspiration (creativepool.com).
- Pinterest: Discover design ideas via collaborative boards like "Graphic Design Inspiration."
- UX Mastery Community: Supportive space for UX and graphic designers (community.uxmastery.com).
- Facebook Groups: Join Graphic Design Inspiration, Logo Geek Community, The Futur Pro Group, Design Cuts, and Typography Enthusiasts for sharing and learning.

By joining these groups, you can participate in discussions, share designs, get constructive feedback, and gain inspiration from other designers.

Don't hesitate to share your design files and ask for detailed advice. Accept criticism gracefully and use it as a tool to refine your skills. Constructive feedback can help you identify your weaknesses and turn them into strengths.

Staying Consistent and Motivated

Progress in graphic design requires dedication, consistent practice, and a positive mindset. Don't be discouraged by setbacks or criticism; instead, use them as opportunities to grow. Trust in your ability to succeed, and remain committed to your learning journey.

The key to mastering graphic design is to practice consistently and invest your time wisely. As you continue to refine your skills and expand your knowledge, you'll notice steady improvement in the quality of your work.

Graphic design is a skill that requires patience, creativity, and determination. By utilizing the wealth of resources available online, joining supportive communities, and dedicating yourself to regular practice, you'll be able to progress quickly and achieve your goals.

Insha'Allah, with hard work and persistence, you'll not only master graphic design but also build a rewarding career in the field. Keep learning, keep practicing, and most importantly, keep believing in your ability to succeed.

Digital Marketing

In today's modern world, effective promotion is essential for business success. With the evolution of technology, marketing strategies have become more advanced. Utilizing digital platforms for promotion is known as digital marketing. Gone are the days when businesses needed loudspeakers to announce their services; now, a Facebook page is enough to start marketing. People involved in such marketing activities are called digital marketers.

To succeed in digital marketing, you need five key skills: research, using tools, presentation, content creation, and selling. Almost every brand, big or small, invests in digital marketing as online interactions now outpace offline ones. This has created high demand for digital marketers, leading to plenty of job opportunities worldwide. Digital marketing has been a vital part of business for years, and its importance keeps growing, with freelancing platforms offering many opportunities for professionals in this field.

Digital marketing is a broad field, and most marketers focus on one or two areas. For example, some are experts in SEO, while others specialize in social media or email marketing. It's not realistic to master everything at once. An email marketer doesn't need to be an SEO expert, and the same goes the other way. Each plays an important role in the digital marketing world.

There are many online resources about becoming a successful digital marketer, but little guidance on practicing it in a halal way. As a Muslim digital marketer, it's important to ensure the businesses you promote are involved in halal activities. Promoting haram products or working for interest-based institutions can make your income invalid.

It's essential to ensure honesty and transparency in your marketing efforts. Avoid using false information or creating misleading content in any campaign. Make sure your work aligns with ethical practices and avoids prohibited elements, such as music or female models, which go against Islamic principles.

For example, if you are running a Facebook ad campaign, ensure the ad content is truthful and promotes a halal product or service. Similarly, if you're working on YouTube SEO or designing video thumbnails, first verify that the channel's content is halal. You wouldn't want your work to support or promote anything that conflicts with your values.

Freelancing – In Search Of Halal Income

In the international market, there are many halal-focused businesses looking for digital marketers. For instance, you could manage the social media of an Islamic bookstore, run email campaigns for a modest fashion brand, or optimize the SEO of a halal food delivery service. These types of projects not only provide income but also allow you to work with businesses that align with your faith.

It's important to research before taking on projects. Understand the client's business, and if you're unsure about their product or content, ask questions. Being transparent shows your commitment to ethical work, and most clients will respect that.

Digital marketing offers many opportunities, like social media management, Google Ads, and content marketing. While it can be very rewarding, choosing halal projects brings peace of mind. You'll know your work helps businesses grow while staying true to your values.

Stay true to your values and show honesty in your work. This builds trust with clients and makes you stand out as someone who values ethics and quality. With effort and patience, you'll find many halal projects to succeed in, Insha'Allah.

The Prophet Muhammad ﷺ said,

"Those who create images in the likeness of Allah's creation will face the severest punishment on the Day of Judgment." [8]

When working with clients on digital marketing projects, thoroughly understand their business and the type of campaigns they want to run. Only accept projects that align with halal principles.

Roadmap to Learning Digital Marketing

Here's a step-by-step roadmap to guide your learning journey:

Start with the Basics

- What is Digital Marketing?
- Key components and their functions
- Target audience, buyer personas, and funnels

Explore SEO

---

[8] Bukhari & Muslim

Freelancing – In Search Of Halal Income

- Search engine functionality
- Keyword research
- On-page and technical SEO
- Backlink building

Social Media Marketing

- Social media algorithms (Facebook, Instagram, LinkedIn)
- Content creation
- Campaign scheduling

Email Marketing

- Building and segmenting email lists
- Crafting campaigns and subject lines
- Metrics: open rates, conversions

Paid Advertising

- Platforms: Google Ads, Facebook Ads. Budget setting and audience targeting
- Campaign optimization

Analytics

- Google Analytics and tracking tools
- Campaign performance metrics, Report generation and analysis

Build a Portfolio

- Create a portfolio showcasing your work, such as blog posts, campaign results, or case studies.
- Work on small projects or internships to gain hands-on experience.

Earning a halal livelihood is crucial in our lives. Since digital marketing encompasses diverse tasks, there is ample room for distinguishing between halal and haram. If you are cautious and informed from the start, earning halal income becomes much easier. Having someone to guide you during your learning phase on what's halal and what's not will set you on the right path.

Content Writing and Translation

In today's internet age, many businesses use content marketing to promote their products or services online. Quality content is needed for everything, from building a website to running marketing campaigns.

To write on any topic, you must first thoroughly understand the subject and learn what kind of content people prefer to read. For instance, if you're writing to promote a product, you need to identify the keywords people use to search for that product and incorporate them effectively into your writing.

Content writing includes many tasks like web content writing, affiliate content writing, technical writing, general blog writing, e-book writing, product description writing, academic writing, rewriting, proofreading, press release writing, CV writing, translation, transcription, news content writing, and social media post writing.

Today, almost every industry or business requires professional content writing. As a result, skilled content writers are in high demand. A professional content writer can charge up to $150 for a 2000-word article, depending on the article's complexity and client preferences. [9]

For example, a Bangladeshi content writer on Upwork charged $150 per hour for a project in October-November 2021 and earned $3,610 in just one month. [10]

If you have good knowledge of contemporary topics and strong English skills, you can pursue content writing as a career. However, it's crucial never to include false or speculative information in your writing. Islam emphasizes honesty, and deception is strictly prohibited.

For instance, if someone asks you to write a review of the top 10 mobile phones, and you submit a list based on assumptions or biased suggestions from a client, it could mislead potential buyers. If someone buys a phone from your list assuming it's one of the best, and later discovers it wasn't, you'd be accountable

---

[9] https://iwriter.com/pricing
[10] https://www.upwork.com/freelancers/~01eccb2217db9bfd99

for misleading them.

The Prophet Muhammad ﷺ said,

"Whoever cheats is not one of us." [11]

Thus, ensure your content is realistic and genuinely beneficial to readers. Avoid writing on haram topics such as promoting music or prohibited products.

Content writing is not limited to corporate projects; individuals also frequently hire writers. Many Facebook groups actively hire content writers for various tasks. If you're a writer, start with one or two small projects before committing to long-term contracts. This approach allows both parties to understand each other's work style and reliability, reducing the risk of misunderstandings.

Plagiarizing content from other sources and publishing it under your name is unethical. Instead, conduct thorough research, read articles written by others on the same topic, and craft your content uniquely. By taking inspiration from others and presenting the information in your voice, you'll create valuable content while respecting intellectual property.

How to Learn Content Writing and Translation?

Content writing is a natural skill, but it can be honed with practice. Everyone's writing style is different, which is perfectly normal. To develop this skill, you must read extensively. Reading introduces you to new ideas and enhances your understanding. When you encounter a new topic, research it thoroughly. The more you learn about a subject, the easier it becomes to write about it.

If you're just starting, publish short articles on blogs or social media platforms. Pay attention to thematic articles and gradually improve your writing skills. Make it a habit to write something every day, whether on your Facebook wall or a blog. This consistent practice will sharpen your skills and establish your credibility as a writer.

To secure work, showcase your writing samples or portfolio when bidding on projects in marketplaces. A strong portfolio increases your chances of landing assignments.

---

[11] Sahih Muslim

What is Translation Work?

Translation involves converting content from one language to another. For instance, you might have come across websites available in multiple languages, where separate content is created for each language. Translation is often required for multilingual websites and is a common task in online marketplaces. Clients may seek translations of English content into French or vice versa. Similarly, there is demand for translators in languages like Arabic, German, Portuguese, Chinese, and Russian.

However, translation work in Bengali is limited on online platforms as the language is predominantly used in Bangladesh and the Indian state of West Bengal. To engage in translation freelancing, it's essential to have proficiency in at least one popular foreign language to secure work and earn halal income.

Arabic-English Translation

Fixed-price - Expert - Est. Budget: $80 - Posted 7 hours ago

Translation needed. Technical language. Cannot use google translate. Roughly 1249 words.

Proposals: 20 to 50

⊘ Payment verified ★★★★ $1k+ spent ⦿ United Kingdom

For example, on the Upwork marketplace, a UK client may post a job to translate Arabic content into English, offering $80 to translate a 1,249-word article. The client explicitly states that translations using tools like Google Translate will not be accepted. This highlights the importance of accurate, professional translation skills, as clients can easily use such tools themselves but seek human translators for precision.

Translate English to Arabic

Fixed-price - Intermediate - Est. Budget: $50 - Posted 8 days ago

The document is about Data, and the documents contains more 50 slide.

Proposals: 50+

⊘ Payment unverified $0 spent ⦿ Saudi Arabia

Similarly, a Saudi Arabian client might post a job to translate 50 slides from English to Arabic, with a budget of $50. Translation projects like these are frequently posted by clients from Arab countries on platforms like Upwork and others.

For students of madrasas (Islamic education) who wish to explore freelancing, translation jobs can be an excellent starting point. Their familiarity with languages such as Arabic, Persian, Urdu, or even other regional or Islamic languages, positions them uniquely to excel in this field. With a strong command of these languages and an understanding of cultural nuances, they can offer valuable services to clients across the globe.

The international market offers countless opportunities for translation work. Clients often require translations for:

- Religious texts, such as Quranic translations, Hadith compilations, or Islamic books.
- Academic papers or research related to Islamic studies.
- Historical manuscripts in Arabic or Persian for universities or cultural organizations.
- Subtitling for Islamic lectures, documentaries, or educational content.

Platforms like Upwork, Fiverr, and Freelancer regularly feature translation projects that require knowledge of these languages. For example:

- An academic institution may need assistance translating a thesis from Arabic to English.
- A publishing house might require an Urdu translation of a popular Islamic book for their audience.
- Non-profit organizations promoting Islamic education may need bilingual support to translate brochures, websites, or promotional materials.

Beyond Islamic content, their language skills can also open doors to broader opportunities. For instance:

- Translating business documents for companies in regions where these languages are widely spoken.
- Assisting in localization projects for software, websites, or apps targeting Arabic or Urdu-speaking markets.
- Providing interpretation services for international events or online conferences.

To succeed internationally, madrasa students can focus on developing complementary skills like proficiency in English, which will help bridge the gap between clients and target audiences. Tools like CAT (Computer-Assisted

Translation) software or platforms such as MemoQ and Trados can enhance their efficiency and accuracy in handling professional projects.

They can also create portfolios showcasing their work, such as translations of sample paragraphs from classical texts or multilingual blog posts. This builds credibility and demonstrates their expertise to clients.

Freelancing not only offers a halal and flexible way to earn but also allows madrasa students to contribute meaningfully to preserving and promoting Islamic knowledge globally. By leveraging their linguistic and cultural strengths, they can access a wide array of projects, connect with clients internationally, and build a successful freelancing career while staying true to their Islamic values. Insha'Allah, this path can lead to both personal and professional growth.

UI & UX Design

UI is the abbreviation for User Interface, which refers to the system enabling interaction between computers and humans. Simply put, everything visible on a screen that facilitates this interaction falls under UI. Designing these visual elements involves the use of colors, shapes, patterns, and more, and is called UI design.

On the other hand, UX stands for User Experience, focusing on ensuring that the user's interaction with the design is smooth and pleasant. A good user experience ensures customer satisfaction and enhances their engagement.

In Bangladesh, mid-level designers earn between 15,000 to 30,000 BDT, while experienced designers can make 40,000 to 80,000 BDT or more. With 2-3 years of experience, some designers earn over 100,000 BDT. Freelancers on marketplaces can earn $1,000–$1,500 monthly, depending on their skill level and portfolio quality.

Designing is Brain Work

Designing requires mental effort rather than physical labor. It involves creative thinking and a calm mind to bring ideas to life. Without patience and passion for design, progressing in this field can be challenging.

Software for UI Design

UI design typically uses software like Figma, Sketch, and Adobe XD. Among these, Figma is highly recommended for beginners as it is free and user-friendly. To learn design effectively, you need to explore how to use the software, install plugins, and utilize them for various tasks. Tutorials on platforms like YouTube can provide excellent guidance.

Mastering the Tools

If you choose Figma, familiarize yourself with its tools, plugin installation, and their functionalities. Watching step-by-step tutorials will help you understand the entire design process.

Key Topics to Learn in UI Design

- User Interface (UI) Design Principles
- Layout and Grid
- Typography (Typeface)
- Alignment
- Dominance with Size, Negative Space, and Contrast
- Image Selection
- Color Theory
- UX Laws (e.g., Hick's Law, Fitts's Law, etc.)
- Wireframing
- Prototyping

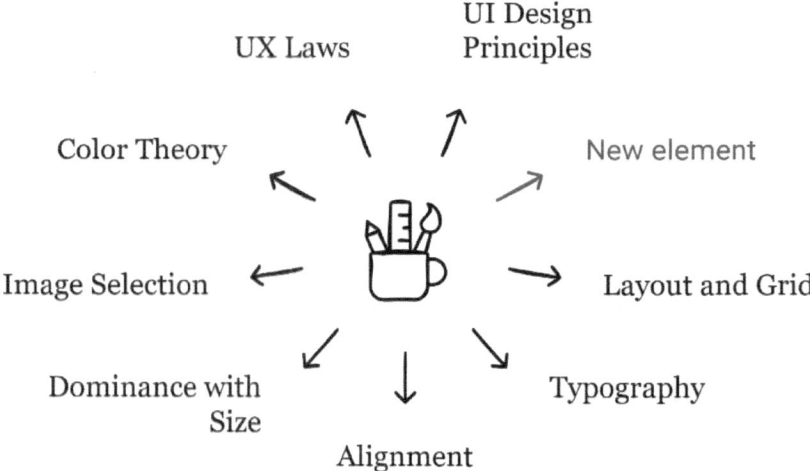

Learning these topics will provide a strong foundation in UI design and prepare you to work professionally. Regular practice and exploring design inspirations will further enhance your skills.

Platforms like Medium, Dribbble, and Behance can provide design inspiration and help you showcase your work. Facebook groups such as *Be Designer*, *Do Halal Design (DHD)*, and *Halal Graphic Land (HGL)* can connect you with clients and provide feedback.

Marketplaces have a high demand for UI designers, with frequent job postings. For example, a Canadian client on Upwork might post a job for an 8-10 page hosting website design. Having relevant samples increases your chances of getting hired.

> **UI/UX Designer To Design Wordpress Hosting Business Website**
>
> Hourly - Expert - Est. Time: 1 to 3 months, Less than 30 hrs/week - Posted 8 days ago
>
> Looking for a talented and experienced ui/ux designer to design a Wordpress hosting business website for me. The total size of the website will be about 8-10 pages.
>
> I'm interested in working with someone who has experience in designing a hosting business or an agency website.
>
> I have a developer already. Just looking for a website designer now. **less**
>
> ✔ Payment verified   ★★★★★ $20k+ spent   📍 Canada

If you already have prior experience designing hosting-related websites, submitting samples alongside your bid can increase your chances of securing the job. Clients often prioritize experienced designers for their projects, as evident in this job post.

The principles for earning halal income, as discussed in the Graphics Design chapter, are equally applicable here. There is no need to repeat those guidelines separately.

Web Development

Web development refers to creating or developing websites using client-side and server-side programming languages based on a design. It involves tasks from structuring a website to making it live on the internet. A web developer is someone who handles these responsibilities.

Being a successful web developer opens up numerous online opportunities. However, relying solely on basic HTML and CSS knowledge might lead to disappointment when seeking work in marketplaces. Therefore, learning PHP and JavaScript, particularly frameworks like AngularJS, Next.js, Vue.js, React.js, Node.js, or Svelte, is essential. If you know HTML and CSS and master one of these JavaScript frameworks, you can easily work as a front-end developer. As web development involves programming, investing sufficient time in learning is crucial.

Start by learning HTML to structure websites and CSS for styling. After gaining solid knowledge of HTML and CSS, explore frameworks like Bootstrap, Tailwind CSS, or Foundation to organize work better and reduce development time.

Avoid Learning Everything at Once

When learning web development, don't try to learn everything at once. Start step by step. Otherwise, you might end up learning nothing thoroughly. Remember, all aspects of web development might be useful eventually, but not everything is necessary in the beginning. Focus on the basics first and build gradually.

Keep the Passion for Learning Alive

Learning web development just for the sake of earning money or securing a job is not enough. Instead, enter the world of programming with a genuine love for the craft. Many people hear that web development is a lucrative career and start learning it, but they lose interest after a while. To succeed, you must remain patient and persistent.

Some people start with great enthusiasm but fail to maintain it, eventually giving up. Stay motivated and keep your passion for learning alive to overcome these challenges.

Halal Income Opportunities in Web Development

A successful web developer has various halal earning opportunities. Below are some key avenues:

- Working in Local and International Software Companies
- Working as a Freelance Web Developer on Various Marketplaces

- Starting Your Own Startup Software Company
- Selling Products (Themes, Templates, Plugins)
- Earning Through Website Flipping
- Earning Through Affiliate Marketing

By focusing on these areas and maintaining an ethical and halal approach, you can build a successful career in web development.

Working in Local and International Software Companies

Currently, there are many small and large software companies in the country that regularly hire web developers. If you acquire strong skills, you can create opportunities to work in these companies. To search for jobs, you can visit platforms like Facebook, LinkedIn, and BDJobs (For Bangaldesh).

When choosing a workplace, don't just focus on the company's size. Instead, consider the **piety (deen-dari)** of the company's owner and the working environment. A large company may lack facilities for offering prayers on time or may not provide a conducive environment for Islamic practices.

Alhamdulillah, most companies do have arrangements for prayers. Working under a devout Muslim owner will make it easier for you to perform your duties, as they are likely to ensure their work aligns with halal principles and will guide their employees accordingly. This will foster a positive and ethical work environment.

Working as a Freelance Web Developer on Various Marketplaces

Among freelance marketplaces, Fiverr.com is relatively easier for beginners to get work. If you are ready to start freelancing, Fiverr can be a good starting point. Additionally, you can explore other platforms like Upwork.com, Freelancer.com, PeoplePerHour.com, and Guru.com to work as a web developer.

A freelancer can create accounts on one or multiple marketplaces. However, it's important to note that creating multiple accounts on the same marketplace is not allowed and could result in account suspension.

Starting Your Own Startup Software Company

Establishing a startup software company might not be easy for everyone, but with Allah's will, you can start on a small scale. I recommend beginning modestly, as this will help you gain experience that can be useful when expanding later. For example, one of the most successful bangladeshi local startups, **JoomShaper**, started in 2010 with just two employees. Most successful startups worldwide begin on a small scale.

Selling Products (Themes, Templates, Plugins)

You can sell web development-related products through your own website or via product-selling marketplaces like **Envato**, **TemplateMonster**, **Creative Market**, or **Codester**. These platforms require a commission or fee for selling your products, such as website templates, themes, or plugins. Alternatively, you can sell directly from your website, avoiding commission fees.

This approach also gives you the freedom to use **halal content** and create products that align with your values. Many developers use inappropriate images, such as models in their designs, either unknowingly or without concern. However, it's important to avoid this practice, even if it might seem to increase sales, as our sustenance (rizq) is predetermined, and there is no need to earn it through prohibited means.

Earning Through Website Flipping

Many people are unfamiliar with website flipping, yet it's a lucrative business where you create websites and sell them to others. As a web developer, this can be relatively easier for you. However, along with development skills, you will need strong market research and marketing knowledge to select suitable websites for flipping.

Earning Through Affiliate Marketing

Affiliate marketing involves earning a commission by promoting and selling products or services through your unique referral link. As a web developer, you can leverage your own website to engage in affiliate marketing and generate income. This allows you to monetize your skills and platform effectively while reaching a broad audience.

However, it is crucial to ensure that both the products you promote and the methods you use comply with Islamic principles. This means avoiding any association with prohibited (haram) products, such as items that conflict with Islamic values, and refraining from using misleading or false information in your marketing efforts. Transparency and honesty should be the foundation of your approach, ensuring that the earnings are pure and permissible.

To maintain compliance with Islamic guidelines, it is advisable to consult a knowledgeable and pious Mufti when selecting products or affiliate programs. This step helps ensure that the choices you make align with Shariah, providing you with peace of mind and fostering trust among your audience. By upholding these principles, you can build a reputable affiliate marketing strategy that not only benefits your income but also reflects your commitment to ethical and halal business practices.

As a web developer, there are ample opportunities to work on the mentioned areas in a halal way.

Website Flipping

Website flipping is an online business model where you create a new website, spend a few months building its traffic, and once the website starts generating income, you sell it. Through this process, it is possible to sell a website for 5–10 times or even more than its monthly revenue.

This business is somewhat similar to real estate, where land is chosen, a house is built on it to increase its value, and then it is sold at a higher price. Similarly, in website flipping, a website is created, enhanced with various features, and made to generate income before selling it for a profit. Here, the website itself becomes a sellable product.

Just as a real estate entrepreneur evaluates which location would make it easier to sell a property, a website flipper must think about the type of websites that are in demand and can be sold easily. Typically, blogs, magazines, news websites, e-commerce sites, and niche-based review websites are the most popular for website flipping.

Some Halal Categories for Websites

The following categories of halal websites are commonly sold:

1. E-commerce
2. Blogs, directory websites, forums
3. Marketplaces
4. Software/service-based websites

By focusing on these categories, you can ensure that your website flipping business aligns with Islamic principles while maximizing profitability.

1. E-Commerce:

E-commerce websites often include platforms for selling digital products, affiliate-based sites, or Shopify-related websites. If you wish to work on such websites, the best approach is to focus on building a site for selling your own products. For websites involving digital products, you must ensure that no haram items are being traded.

Dropshipping websites are not permissible because you do not own the product. In dropshipping, you display someone else's product on your website and sell it without taking ownership. According to Shariah, a product cannot be sold without taking possession of it. One of the core principles of Shariah is that profit can only be earned when the item is under the seller's ownership and responsibility. Profiting without bearing responsibility is not permissible.

The Prophet Muhammad (ﷺ) forbade selling something that is not in one's possession. The essence of this principle is that profit is only justified when one takes responsibility and bears the risk of gain or loss.

However, if you own an e-commerce website where you sell your products and then decide to sell that website, there is no issue with that. Shariah dictates that no product can be sold before it is owned or under the seller's possession. Without ownership, transferring the product to the buyer is not feasible, and such a sale holds no value.

Ibn Abbas (RA) narrated: The Prophet (ﷺ) forbade selling foodstuffs before acquiring possession of them. Ibn Abbas said, "I consider this rule applicable to all things."

2. Blogs, Directory Websites, and Forums:

These types of websites can cover a wide range of topics. However, it is essential to ensure that the content is not related to any haram subjects. Blogs and forums are often monetized, so it is crucial to ensure that the monetization methods are halal.

For instance:

- Avoid creating blogs with false or speculative information.
- If advertisements are placed on the website, ensure they do not feature music or images of immodestly dressed individuals.

Allah says in the Qur'an:

"And cooperate in righteousness and piety, but do not cooperate in sin and aggression. And fear Allah; indeed, Allah is severe in penalty."

3. Marketplace:

A marketplace is a platform where products or services are bought and sold. For example, amazon.com is a website where products are sold, making it an example of an e-commerce marketplace. Similarly, Upwork is a platform where freelancers sell their services, which is an example of a service-based marketplace.

A notable example is Monerojobs.com, which was sold for $5,000 on Flippa.com. It was a job marketplace website. Such marketplaces can be created and sold for profit.

4. Software/Service-Based Websites:

You can create and sell a website based on software or services, or one related to a startup business. These types of websites are in high demand and can generate significant revenue if built and marketed effectively.

List of some Software/Service-Based Websites Sold on Flippa.com

Website Name	Selling Price
perfectprospect.io	$25,000
timezap.io	$15,000
SurviveOnAnyBudget.com	$10,501
20dishes.com	$10,000
Polls.io	$5,000

Steps for Website Flipping

Step 1: Purchase a Domain or Website

If you are building the entire website from scratch, start by purchasing a domain and then develop the website on that domain. Alternatively, if you are buying a ready-made website, carefully review its analytics and other metrics before making a purchase to ensure its potential for success.

Step 2: Increase Website Traffic

Whether you have created or purchased the website, the next step is to increase its traffic. To do this, regularly add quality content to the website and implement both on-page and off-page SEO techniques. There are many tutorials on YouTube and Google about increasing website traffic through SEO.

As traffic grows and the website starts generating income, it will become suitable for selling.

Step 3: Sell the Website

There are many platforms available for selling websites or domains. Popular options include Flippa, Trademysite, Afternic, Freemarket, Digital Point Forum, Web Hosting Talk, and Empire Flippers. Among these, Flippa.com is the most widely recognized and used for website flipping.

Key Points for Halal Earnings Through Website Flipping

To ensure halal earnings in website flipping, consider the following:

- **Source of Income**: Verify how the website generates income.
- **Content**: Ensure that the website's content is halal and does not involve anything prohibited.
- **Products or Services**: Make sure the products or services sold on the website are halal.
- **Marketing Methods**: Confirm that the marketing techniques are halal and free from deceit or falsehood.
- **Honesty**: Avoid any form of dishonesty or fraud in the process.

By adhering to these principles, you can ensure that your earnings are halal, Insha'Allah.

App Development

In our daily lives, we use various devices, and one of the most prominent among them is the mobile phone. Among different types of mobiles, Android devices are the most popular. One key reason for this popularity is the availability and ease of use of various applications on Android devices, alongside other features. Every day, we use various apps on our phones to make life more convenient. For example, we might use Google Maps for navigating unfamiliar locations, apps like Uber Eats, DoorDash, or Grubhub to order food when hosting guests, and government apps like MySejahtera or COVID Certificate to register for vaccinations.

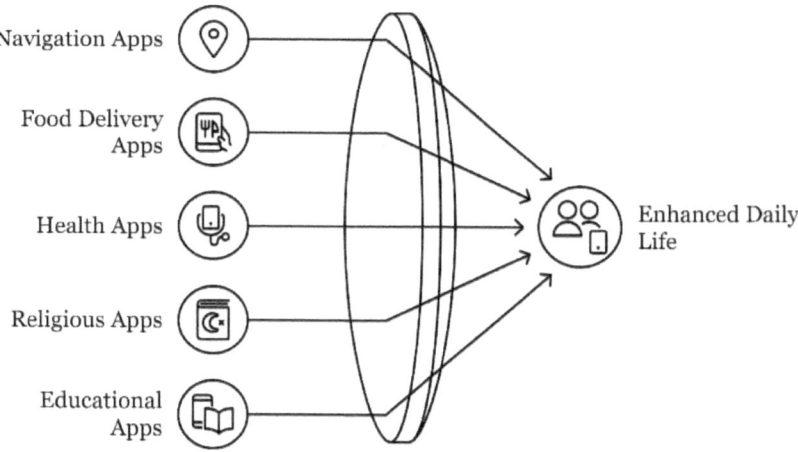

Not only that, mobile apps are also widely used for religious purposes. For instance, while waiting for congregational prayers at the mosque, we can use Quran apps to recite verses. Additionally, we can listen to recitations by renowned Qaris worldwide to improve our own. Mobile apps also provide access to a wealth of Islamic resources, including Tafsir of the Quran, collections of authentic Hadith, and other educational materials, making it easier to engage in religious study and self-improvement.

With advancements in technology, our reliance on apps in daily life is increasing. Apps have made our lives easier and more comfortable. Behind every app is someone who develops it. Hence, app development can be a smart career choice.

Popular Mobile Platforms

Currently, the two most popular mobile operating systems are Android and iOS. Other operating systems like Symbian, Blackberry OS, Windows OS, Palm OS, MeeGo, and BADA were once well-known but are now less prevalent. Most mobile app development today is focused on Android and iOS platforms.

Becoming an App Developer

You don't necessarily need a formal degree in computer science or programming to become an app developer, although academic knowledge can make the process easier. Anyone with interest and dedication can become an app developer. Since app development is entirely programming-based, having a strong understanding of programming is crucial. Once you have a good grasp of programming, you can proceed to learn app development thoroughly.

Spending 6–8 hours a day learning app development can help you become a reasonably skilled app developer within a year. However, to become a market-ready developer capable of working on high-quality projects, more time and effort will be required. The time frame varies depending on individual learning speed and method.

For free resources, you can explore YouTube tutorials, blogs, or online courses. Additionally, there are many Bengali resources available online for learning app development. Google's Android Developers Portal (developer.android.com) also provides essential resources for developers.

How to Earn Through App Development

If you master app development, you can find various ways to earn. Here are five halal ways to earn through app development:

- Working as an app developer on freelancing marketplaces.
- Selling paid apps on platforms like the Play Store or Apple Store.
- Selling apps on marketplaces like Envato and others.
- Creating service-based apps and selling subscriptions.
- Working for local companies or software firms.

Earning Through Ads and Halal Considerations

Some developers earn by creating free apps and monetizing them through ads.

However, strict guidelines must be followed to ensure the ads comply with Islamic principles:

- Ads should not feature female models or anything un-Islamic.
- Ads should not promote haram or sinful activities.

If you use ad services like Google AdSense or AdMob, you have limited control over the types of ads displayed in your app. Ads may include images, videos, or music that are inappropriate, making you indirectly complicit in haram activities. Therefore, caution is essential. It's advisable to consult a knowledgeable Mufti with details of your work to get a proper fatwa.

Cautions and Alternative Income Models

Many aspiring developers focus on earning through Google AdSense, assuming that more installs mean more ad views and, subsequently, more income. Unfortunately, many Islamic apps on the Play Store are filled with un-Islamic ads. On the other hand, some apps earn revenue through sponsorships or subscriptions without relying on ads, which is a permissible method.

If you can create an innovative app that solves a significant problem or serves an essential purpose, people will be willing to pay for it.

Final Thoughts

For those planning to learn app development or build a career in this field, it is crucial to distinguish between halal and haram methods. By following these guidelines, you can ensure that your work and income align with Islamic principles.

Data Processing

Data processing involves transforming raw data into meaningful information through analysis, organization, and other methods. In online marketplaces, various types of work related to data are available, such as Data Mining & Scraping, Formulas & Macros, Automations, Data Analytics, Data Visualization, Data Engineering, and Data Science. Data processing is not limited to basic data entry tasks; it encompasses much more complex and specialized areas.

On platforms like Fiverr, many freelancers provide services related to data processing. Some work on Excel automation, while others handle web scraping, data mining, and data extraction. Others focus on data statistics and analysis, and some even perform data engineering tasks using Python scripts.

For example, imagine you have a large dataset that needs to be formatted or visualized as a report. Doing this task manually would take a lot of time and may lead to errors. However, using a script or an automated process ensures that the task is completed quickly and accurately. Platforms like Indeed, SimplyHired, and Upwork frequently post jobs for data scientists and data engineers. Based on an analysis of 3,100 salaries, the average monthly salary of a data engineer in the United States was $8,289 as of November 22, 2021. By May 2024, after analyzing 6,800 salaries, the average monthly salary had increased to $9,097. This shows a consistent growth in this sector's earning potential and workforce demand.

How to Start Working in Data Processing

It is clear that with the right skills, you can earn a lucrative income by engaging in data processing tasks. In today's competitive job market, possessing knowledge in areas such as Python programming, Excel VBA, or Excel Macros opens the door to a wide range of opportunities. These skills enable you to handle diverse data-related projects, from creating automated workflows to conducting complex data analysis. Online marketplaces like Upwork, Fiverr, and Freelancer host countless job postings for professionals with expertise in these areas, offering you the chance to secure work and grow your portfolio. The Role of AI in Data Processing

With the advent of **Artificial Intelligence (AI)**, many data processing tasks are now being automated. While AI has replaced some jobs, it has also created opportunities for complex and advanced data processing tasks. Automation has made it possible to complete tasks that used to take hours in mere moments. Tasks like analyzing large datasets, which would take humans a long time, can now be done instantly using AI.

By advancing your data processing skills towards data engineering, you can create innovative solutions and keep up with the industry's demands. Freelance marketplaces continue to have a high demand for data science professionals, and new jobs in this category are being posted regularly.

Key Considerations for Halal Work

When working in the field of data processing, it is essential to ensure that the company or client you are collaborating with operates a halal business. This means that their operations should comply with Islamic principles, avoiding any involvement in haram (prohibited) activities such as selling unlawful products, promoting unethical services, or engaging in activities that go against Shariah. Additionally, you must verify that the company is not involved in interest-based (riba) transactions or practices, which are strictly prohibited in Islam.

For example, if the company operates in sectors like gambling, alcohol, or other industries deemed impermissible, you should refrain from providing services to them. Similarly, if their business model includes interest-based loans or transactions, your contribution to such work would also be considered non-compliant with Islamic ethics. This scrutiny is not only vital for ensuring that your income is halal but also aligns your professional activities with your faith and values.

To uphold these principles, it is advisable to conduct due diligence before accepting any project. This could involve researching the company's background, reviewing their business operations, or even directly asking about their compliance with halal business practices. If you are unsure, consulting a knowledgeable Mufti or Islamic scholar can provide clarity and help you make an informed decision.

By adhering to these ethical standards and continuously developing your skills in areas like data visualization, data analysis, or data engineering, you can build a rewarding career in data processing. This approach not only ensures that your income is pure and permissible but also strengthens your professional reputation as someone committed to integrity and ethical excellence.

Virtual Assistant

The virtual world is a space where people connect with one another using computers, mobile devices, and other digital tools. Working as a virtual assistant involves providing support to various companies from the comfort of your home using a computer. This allows you to offer services to clients worldwide while staying at home.

Virtual assistant tasks are not limited to a specific set of responsibilities; instead, they vary based on the needs of the company or client. Common job requirements include proficiency in tools like Microsoft Word, Excel, Google Spreadsheets, email handling, and marketing. While the scope of work can differ, it is crucial to decide beforehand what type of services you will provide and search for jobs accordingly.

Common tasks performed by virtual assistants include:

- Responding to clients' emails.
- Updating websites.
- Bookkeeping.
- Business communication.

Freelancing – In Search Of Halal Income

- Managing social media accounts.
- Conducting business research.

Imagine you own a business and are often busy with its operations. You can hire a virtual assistant to maintain your business's social media accounts, answer phone calls, and respond to messages or emails.

Skills Required to Become a Virtual Assistant

To become a virtual assistant, proficiency in English is essential since you will likely work with clients from other countries while operating from your home in Bangladesh (or elsewhere). Without good English skills, effective client communication can be challenging.

Once you are confident in your English abilities, focus on developing skills related to virtual assistant tasks. Start by creating sample work based on the typical responsibilities of a virtual assistant. Use online marketplaces to understand what types of work virtual assistants do and tailor your samples accordingly.

Familiarity with tools like Google Advanced Search, Google Trends, Google News, Google Analytics, Google Maps, Yellow Pages, and social media platforms will give you an edge in securing web research-related jobs. Consistently apply for tasks that match your skills on freelancing platforms. Insha'Allah, you will find your desired job.

Salary for Virtual Assistant Jobs

The average salary for virtual assistant jobs in the United States is $28 per hour,[12] though this rate can vary depending on the level of expertise, experience,

---

[12] https://indeed.com/career/virtual-assistant/salaries

and the nature of the tasks involved. Entry-level virtual assistants who handle basic administrative tasks like email management, scheduling, and data entry typically earn between $15 and $20 per hour.

On the other hand, experienced virtual assistants with specialized skills—such as social media management, graphic design, or bookkeeping—can earn significantly more, often ranging from $30 to $50 per hour or even higher. Some virtual assistants who offer niche services, like project management or technical support, can command premium rates based on their expertise and the value they bring to their clients.

Ethical Considerations

When working as a virtual assistant, it's important to make sure that the tasks you take on align with halal business practices. This means choosing work that is ethical, lawful, and does not support or promote activities that are considered haram (prohibited) in Islam. For example, you should avoid jobs that involve gambling, alcohol promotion, misleading advertisements, or any form of unethical behavior.

Think of it this way: your work reflects not just your skills but also your values. By prioritizing halal opportunities, you ensure that your income is clean, ethical, and in line with Islamic principles. This doesn't just benefit you spiritually but also builds trust with your clients, as they'll see you as someone who values integrity in every task.

If you ever come across a job that seems unclear or questionable, don't hesitate to take a step back and evaluate. It's perfectly fine to ask for details about the nature of the business or consult someone knowledgeable in Islamic rulings to guide you. Remember, it's better to walk away from something that feels wrong than to compromise your principles.

At the same time, being selective doesn't mean limiting your opportunities. The virtual assistant field offers plenty of halal and meaningful work—from helping small businesses grow to managing social media, email communication, and beyond. With the right skills and mindset, you'll find countless opportunities to succeed while staying true to your values.

By sticking to these principles, not only will you earn a halal income, but you'll also feel a sense of peace and fulfillment knowing that your work is ethically sound and spiritually rewarding. And that's the best kind of success, isn't it?

Freelancing – In Search Of Halal Income

Market Research

Research refers to the process of systematic investigation, and it can take various forms. For example, if you are planning to start a business, you might need to research competitors' data, market data, customer data, etc. Freelancers perform these types of tasks in online marketplaces, which are referred to as market research.

Depending on the nature of the work, the rates for market research jobs can vary widely. If you deliver quality work, it is possible to charge over $100 per hour for market research-related tasks.

For instance, while browsing a market research expert's profile on Upwork.com, I found someone who charges $100 per hour and has earned over $300,000 on the platform.

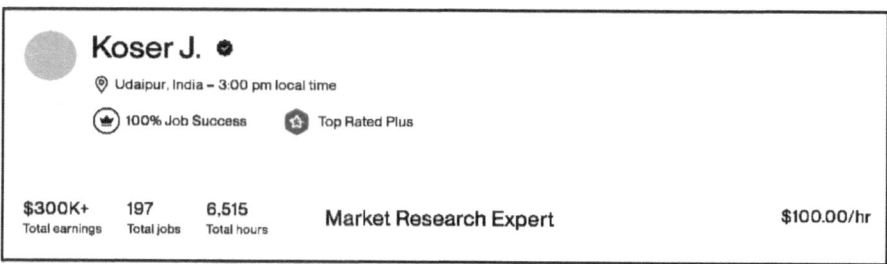

This success didn't happen overnight. The individual has been working in business research and strategy consulting for over 14 years, completing 168 jobs and earning more than $200,000 from a single marketplace. This highlights their dedication and hard work in the field.

According to Indeed.com, the average annual salary of a research assistant in the United States is over $40,000. Companies conduct research on various topics, such as understanding the types of products people are interested in buying and the ones they avoid. Such research helps companies make critical decisions before launching their products in the market.

This research can be conducted both offline and online. After collecting data, it is analyzed, formatted, and presented in a way that supports decision-making. These tasks are typically carried out by research specialists or analysts.

Freelancing – In Search Of Halal Income

On **Fiverr.com**, many freelancers work as market researchers, focusing on tasks such as:

- Market sizing.
- Potential growth analysis.
- Latest trends analysis.
- Consumer behavior analysis.
- Competitor analysis.
- SWOT Analysis (Strengths, Weaknesses, Opportunities, and Threats).

Freelancers often charge between **$300 - $1,000** for preparing comprehensive market research reports for companies.

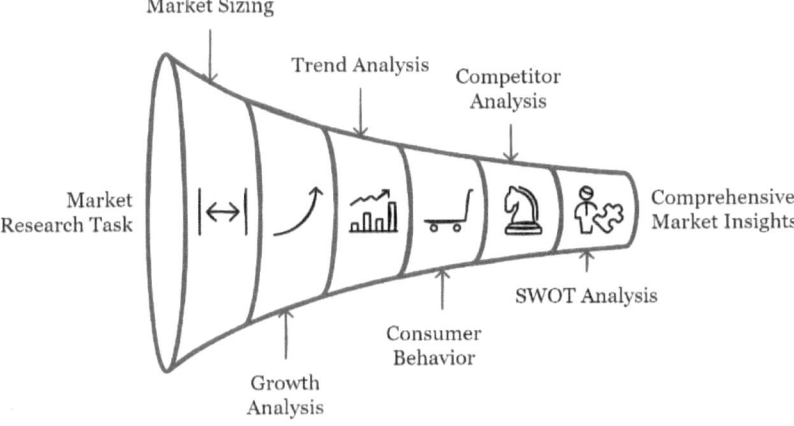

Market Research Process Funnel

Skills Required for Market Research

Market research is a field that demands a combination of analytical and interpersonal skills, making it ideal for individuals who enjoy solving problems and uncovering insights. To excel in this field, having a creative mindset, strong proficiency in English, and a solid understanding of statistics are key prerequisites. These skills enable you to effectively gather, analyze, and present data in ways that help businesses make informed decisions. Additionally, the competition in this field is relatively low compared to other freelancing categories, providing an excellent opportunity for those willing to invest the time and effort to master the craft.

However, excelling in market research is not just about technical skills; it also requires a high level of integrity and professionalism. When working in this category, it is crucial to ensure that the reports you produce are based on accurate, reliable, and verified data. Fabricated or false information can not only damage your reputation but also lead to significant financial and strategic losses for your client. Trust is a cornerstone of this profession, and your success as a market researcher heavily depends on your ability to deliver trustworthy and meaningful insights.

For example, some individuals resort to unethical practices such as using VPNs to generate fake survey responses on unreliable websites. While these shortcuts might seem tempting, they undermine the credibility of the research and can severely harm the client's business. Using such questionable methods not only compromises the quality of your work but also violates ethical standards.

As a Muslim, adhering to honesty and fairness is a religious obligation. Islam teaches us to ensure that our work benefits, rather than harms, the people we serve. When providing market research services, it is your duty to avoid causing harm to the client, whether intentionally or unintentionally. This means going the extra mile to verify your data sources, cross-check your findings, and present conclusions that are as accurate as possible.

Search Engine Optimization (SEO)

Search Engine Optimization, or SEO, is a method used to improve a website's visibility in search engine results. The goal is to have the website or webpage appear at the top of search results, making it easily accessible to users. SEO is not a single task but rather a combination of various techniques and processes that work together to optimize a website's performance.

The primary objective of SEO is to make a website easily discoverable to everyone, increase its popularity, and attract more visitors. When we search for something on Google or another search engine, the search engine displays results based on our query. From these results, we select the most relevant website. SEO is the reason why some websites appear on the first page of search results, ensuring better visibility and higher traffic.

Why is SEO Important for a Website?

Imagine you own a restaurant business and have a website for it. To ensure your customers can easily find your website, you need to optimize it with SEO. When potential customers search for restaurant services, your website will appear in the search results, attracting visitors who can then place orders.

Since there are many websites offering similar services, having your website listed at the top of the search results increases the likelihood of attracting more customers. SEO is essential for achieving this and plays a crucial role in staying competitive in the business landscape.

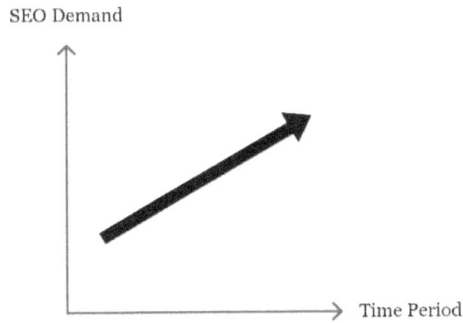

Demand for SEO Work in Marketplaces

SEO-related jobs are posted frequently in online marketplaces, and skilled SEO experts are always in demand. While SEO work is often perceived as having lower rates, experienced professionals can earn significantly more.

	Raihan I.
	Dinajpur Sadar Upazila, Bangladesh - 9:36 am local time
100% Job Success	TOP RATED PLUS
49 Total Jobs	11,525 Total Hours	SEO Expert	SEO Manager	Guest Posting Expert	$50.00/hr

For example, I've seen an SEO expert on Upwork charge $100 per hour, earning $11,000 from a single project. Additionally, a Bangladeshi freelancer working at $50 per hour managed to earn over $33,000 on a project from March to November 2021.

Companies are willing to pay higher rates for skilled SEO experts because they play a vital role in increasing customer engagement and growing the business. Marketplaces always have a steady demand for competent SEO professionals who are capable of delivering results.

Learning SEO

To succeed in SEO, proficiency in English is essential since you will often work with clients from different countries. Effective communication is key to understanding client requirements and delivering quality work.

You can start learning SEO by watching tutorials on YouTube and regularly visiting SEO blogs and forums. These platforms allow you to learn from industry leaders and expand your knowledge.

Recommended Blogs and Forums for Learning SEO

- Moz Blog
- Search Engine Land
- Search Engine Journal
- Search Engine Watch
- Backlinko Blog
- Ahrefs Blog

Freelancing – In Search Of Halal Income

- Warrior Forum
- Digital Point Forums
- Reddit SEO

Platforms for Offering SEO Services

Once you learn SEO, you can offer your services on all major freelancing platforms. Additionally, platforms like SEOClerk.com specialize in SEO-related services, allowing you to sell small, quality services and earn well. Similarly, Fiverr.com is another platform where you can list your SEO services.

Before offering your services, research the types of SEO services others are providing and their pricing. This will help you position yourself effectively in the market.

Ethical Considerations in SEO Work

When working on SEO projects, ensure that the work does not involve haram (prohibited) elements, such as inappropriate visuals, music, or other activities against Islamic principles. If the business or content aligns with Islamic values, the SEO work will be halal, Insha'Allah.

Sometimes, questions arise about working on websites that feature women's images, such as a hospital website showcasing male and female doctors or an e-commerce site selling women's products.

According to Mufti Imdadul Haq:

"Since the images are not part of your work, promoting such websites and working as an SEO specialist for them is permissible. Additionally, if the images are minimal, the earnings will not be entirely haram. However, the individual will still be accountable for their involvement with such images."

If you face any doubts about the nature of a project, seek guidance from a knowledgeable Islamic scholar or Mufti before proceeding. For Islamic rulings, you can also ask questions on platforms like islamweb.

SEO offers an excellent opportunity to earn a halal income, making it an attractive option for individuals seeking a flexible and rewarding career in the digital space. With the increasing demand for skilled SEO professionals across global marketplaces, this field provides ample opportunities to work with businesses from various industries. However, the permissibility of the work depends entirely on the nature of the projects you choose to undertake.

Freelancing – In Search Of Halal Income

As a Muslim, it's important to ensure that the content or business you are optimizing complies with Shariah principles. This means avoiding projects that promote haram (prohibited) activities, such as gambling, alcohol, or unethical content. Even the presence of inappropriate visuals, music, or other elements that conflict with Islamic values must be considered carefully.

For example, if you're working on an e-commerce website selling halal products but featuring images of female models, consult a qualified Islamic scholar to ensure that your involvement in promoting the website is permissible. Many scholars, including Mufti Imdadul Haq, have stated that if the problematic content is not directly part of your work, your overall income may still be halal, though accountability for involvement with such elements remains.

Ethical SEO practices go beyond Shariah compliance. Always ensure your work is honest and transparent. Avoid using black-hat SEO tactics, such as keyword stuffing, buying backlinks, or creating misleading content, as these can damage your professional reputation and compromise your integrity. Instead, focus on providing value by optimizing websites in ways that genuinely improve their usability and visibility.

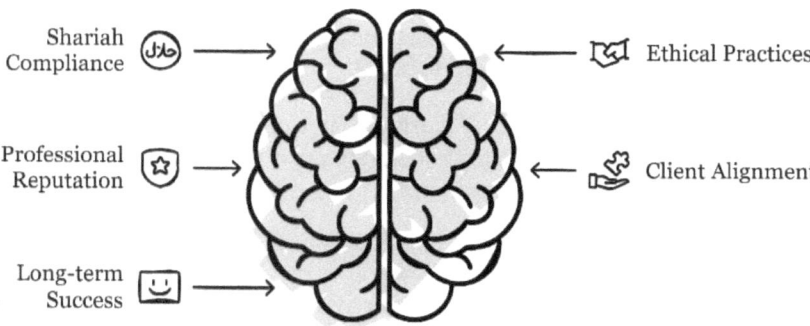

To achieve long-term success in this field, take time to research potential clients and their businesses. Only accept projects that align with your values and principles. If ever in doubt, seek advice from trusted Islamic scholars.

By adhering to ethical and Shariah-compliant practices, you can confidently pursue a career in SEO, knowing that your income is halal and your efforts contribute positively to your clients' success. With dedication and consistent learning, you can build a successful, fulfilling career in this growing industry while staying true to your faith, Insha'Allah.

Customer Support

In today's competitive market, achieving customer satisfaction is essential for any business's growth and reputation. Most corporate organizations have dedicated customer support departments to assist their customers efficiently.

For instance, imagine you want to purchase a product from an e-commerce website, but before buying, you need additional information about the product. In such cases, you would contact the company's hotline number or use their live chat to get the required details. Similarly, after purchasing a product, if any issues arise, you would reach out to their customer support for solutions.

Businesses with direct customer interactions, such as e-commerce platforms or service providers, rely heavily on customer support to maintain their operations. The professionals who assist customers by providing information and solving their issues are known as Customer Support Agents or Customer Service Representatives.

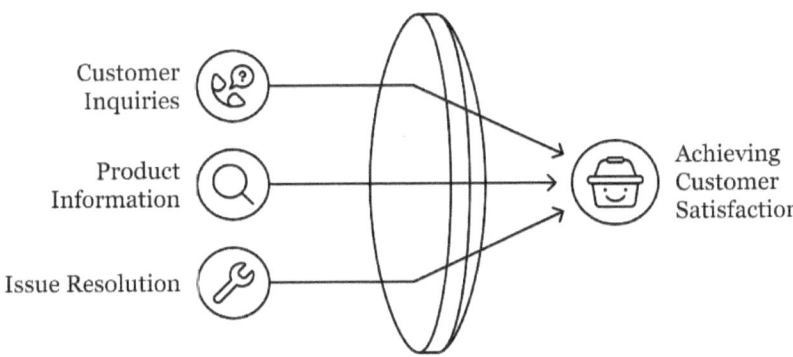

The Role of Customer Support Agents

With the internet making remote work accessible, you can work as a Call Center Agent or Customer Care Representative for businesses around the world, right from the comfort of your home.

Customer support roles encompass a wide variety of tasks, including:

- Order processing and tracking.
- Refund processing and order fulfillment.
- Communicating with suppliers and customers.
- Providing email support and managing live chat.
- Offering direct support through voice calls.

Success in customer service depends on several key skills and qualities. A Customer Care Executive must:

- Have a thorough understanding of the company's products or services.
- Be capable of addressing customer complaints with intelligence and efficiency.
- Listen attentively to customers' concerns and provide appropriate solutions.
- Act as a bridge between the company and its customers, ensuring smooth communication.
- Possess qualities like politeness, patience, quick thinking, and professionalism.

Each customer is different, with unique needs and expectations. Therefore, it is essential to approach every issue with empathy and resolve it with intelligence and tact.

Opportunities in the Global Market

The demand for Customer Support Representatives is high worldwide. Platforms like ZipRecruiter, Indeed, SimplyHired, and Glassdoor frequently post customer service job openings, offering rates between $15 to $50 per hour. Additionally, platforms like LinkedIn provide excellent opportunities for finding similar jobs. To succeed on LinkedIn, create a professional profile showcasing your skills and experience.

Those proficient in English can work for international clients, while individuals fluent in Arabic can cater to clients in Arab countries.

Key Considerations for Ethical Work

When working in customer support, it's crucial to ensure that the business you're assisting is halal. Avoid working for companies that promote haram activities, such as:

- Interest-based banking or financial services.
- Gambling or unethical offers.
- Businesses with haram products or services.

- Female agents should handle voice calls with female customers, and male agents should handle voice calls with male customers, adhering to Islamic guidelines for gender interaction.

For instance, many call centers promote interest-based banking offers, which are prohibited in Islam. Working for such organizations is not permissible. Always prioritize working for halal businesses to ensure that your income is lawful and ethical.

Essential Skills for Success

To excel as a Customer Support Representative, focus on developing the following skills:

- Understand the products or services you're supporting to address customer inquiries effectively.
- Be articulate, polite, and professional in all customer interactions.
- Analyze issues quickly and offer practical solutions.
- Handle diverse customer personalities with understanding and composure.

These qualities not only enhance your efficiency but also contribute to the company's positive reputation.

Customer support is a promising career path that offers flexibility, steady income, and excellent earning potential. With the growing reliance on remote work and online services, opportunities in this field are abundant on platforms like LinkedIn, Upwork, Fiverr, and other freelance job sites. Whether you prefer full-time employment or freelancing, there are countless opportunities available for individuals with the right skills and dedication.

Understanding Shariah Compliance in Customer Support

To ensure that your income remains halal, you must verify the nature of the company you are working for and the products or services they offer. For example, a business promoting ethical products or halal services is suitable, whereas one offering haram financial schemes or unethical activities is not permissible.

If you are ever unsure about the permissibility of a particular job, it is wise to consult a knowledgeable Islamic scholar or refer to trusted Islamic advisory platforms like **ifatwa.info**. A scholar can provide clarity on whether the nature of the work aligns with Islamic principles.

Practical Tips for Maintaining Shariah Compliance

- Before accepting a position, thoroughly research the company's business model, products, and services to ensure they are halal.
- Clearly understand your job responsibilities and ensure they do not involve promoting haram activities, misleading customers, or unethical practices.
- For roles involving live chat, email, or phone support, ensure you are not required to handle or promote content that conflicts with Islamic values.
- Regularly seek advice from scholars if you encounter doubts about your work. It's better to clarify issues beforehand than to inadvertently engage in impermissible activities.

Building a Successful and Halal Career

Customer support can be a fulfilling and lucrative career if approached ethically. By honing essential skills such as communication, problem-solving, patience, and product knowledge, you can become a valuable asset to any company. Additionally, by choosing halal businesses and ensuring Shariah compliance, you not only secure a lawful income but also gain the blessings of Allah in your work.

Remember, your intention matters. Strive to use your role in customer support to genuinely help people, resolve their concerns, and contribute to businesses that align with Islamic principles. With hard work, ethical practices, and reliance on Allah, you can build a career that is both rewarding and spiritually fulfilling, Insha'Allah.

Project Management

Project management involves organizing and managing tasks, resources, and people to achieve specific goals within a defined timeline. It is a vital role in many industries, ensuring projects are completed successfully and efficiently by utilizing knowledge, skills, and strategic planning. Freelancers often take on project management tasks remotely for companies around the world.

For instance, imagine you run a digital agency with web developers, graphic designers, digital marketers, SEO experts, and other team members. Managing all of them while focusing on your priorities can become overwhelming. Hiring a **Project Manager** can simplify this process. A Project Manager communicates with the team, tracks progress, provides updates, and ensures deadlines are met.

For example, a graphic designer creating a logo might not know the exact delivery timeline unless communicated by the Project Manager. Similarly, the Project Manager bridges the gap between the client and the team, gathering feedback and providing updates to ensure smooth project execution.

Key Skills and Responsibilities of a Project Manager

A Project Manager's leadership skills and strategic abilities are crucial for ensuring a project's success. They must coordinate with all team members, allocate tasks effectively, and manage resources to complete projects on time.

According to Indeed.com, the average monthly salary for a Project Manager in the United States is $5,226 USD, highlighting the value of this role. Freelancing platforms like Upwork, Fiverr, and LinkedIn also feature numerous opportunities for Project Managers.

To excel as a Project Manager, one must be multi-talented, as the role often involves diverse tasks. For instance:

- Proficiency in using project management tools like Asana, Notion, Trello, Monday.com, ClickUp, and Basecamp is essential.
- Basic knowledge of graphic design (using tools like Canva) and video editing (with tools like CapCut) can provide an added advantage for managing creative projects.

Opportunities in Project Management

Social media platforms like LinkedIn are excellent places to find project management opportunities. Unlike casual platforms like Facebook, LinkedIn allows you to connect with CEOs, HR managers, and directors from prominent global companies who frequently post job openings for Project Managers.

Additionally, freelancing platforms like Upwork are filled with job postings for project management and virtual assistant roles. Many individuals from Bangladesh are already working in these roles for international clients. Graduates with BBA or MBA degrees can utilize their academic knowledge and combine it with technical skills to pursue a fulfilling career in project management.

Tools and Skills for Project Management

To thrive as a Project Manager, you need to master various tools and develop a diverse skill set. Some of the most commonly used tools include:

- Asana, Trello, Monday.com, ClickUp, Basecamp, Zoho Projects (for task and project management).
- Canva (for basic graphic design).
- CapCut (for video editing).

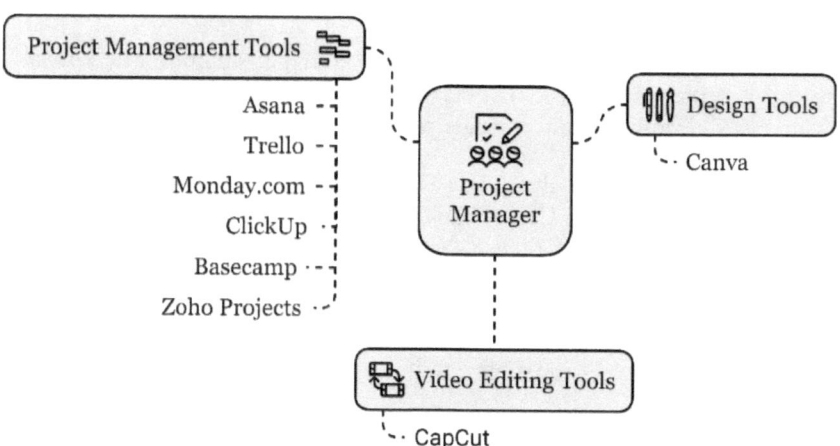

These tools help streamline project workflows, enhance team collaboration, and improve overall efficiency.

In addition to technical skills, soft skills such as communication, problem-solving, time management, and critical thinking are equally important for ensuring project success.

Shariah Compliance in Project Management

As a Muslim, it is vital to ensure that your work aligns with Islamic principles. When selecting projects or clients, always verify that the company engages in halal business practices. Avoid working with companies involved in haram activities, such as:

- Interest-based financial services.
- Gambling or unethical promotions.
- Businesses dealing with haram products or services.

If you're ever in doubt about a project's permissibility, consult a knowledgeable Islamic scholar to clarify the matter. By adhering to Shariah-compliant practices, you can ensure that your income remains halal and your work aligns with your values.

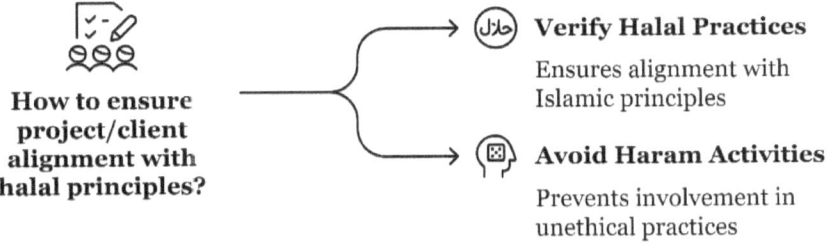

Project management offers a lucrative and dynamic career path for those who enjoy leadership and organization. With the right combination of tools, technical skills, and a commitment to Islamic ethics, you can excel in this field.

By focusing on halal businesses and constantly upgrading your skills, you can build a fulfilling career that not only supports your professional growth but also ensures spiritual peace, Insha'Allah.

Business Consultant

The term **consultant** means an advisor, and a **business consultant** refers to a professional who provides expert advice to help businesses improve and succeed. Many freelancers work as business consultants on online marketplaces, assisting companies by analyzing their current status and offering strategies to achieve their goals.

This career is not for everyone—it requires in-depth knowledge of business operations, management, and strategic planning. Those with a strong understanding of these fields can establish themselves as successful business consultants in the freelance world.

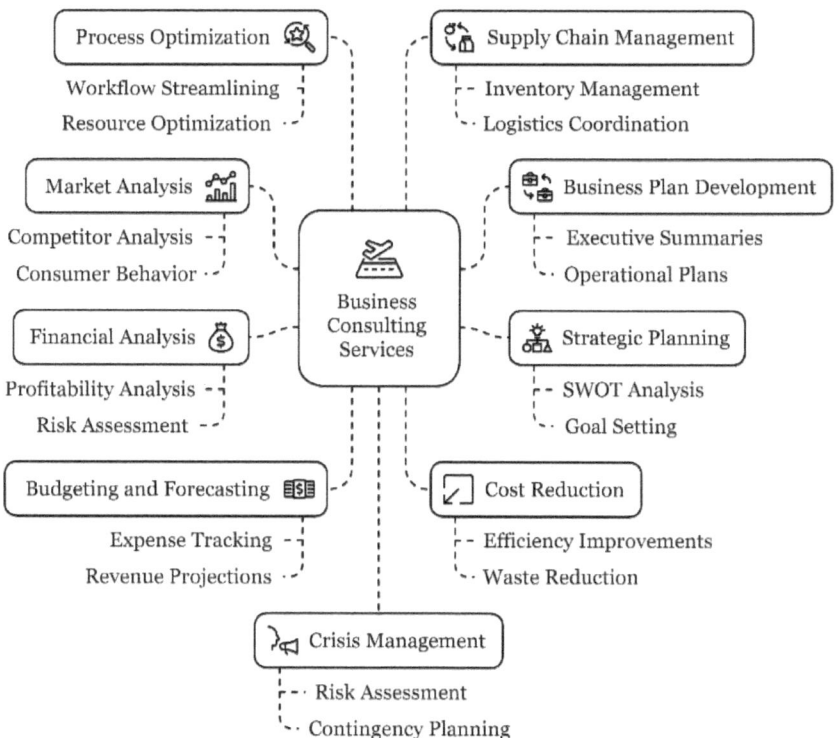

Key services provided by business consultants include Market Analysis,

Freelancing – In Search Of Halal Income

Business Plan Development, Strategic Planning, Financial Analysis, Budgeting and Forecasting, Cost Reduction, Process Optimization, Supply Chain Management, Crisis Management, Startup Consulting, Mentorship, and Funding Strategy.

I came across a seller on Fiverr.com who teaches how to become a successful freelancer. He is a top-rated seller with over a thousand reviews on his profile. Some provide services on how to succeed in business on Amazon, while others offer guidance on managing a new startup business. In this way, various individuals work as business consultants in marketplaces, offering diverse ideas and expertise.

Opportunities for Freelancers

Although the number of freelancers worldwide working as business consultants may vary across regions, there are ample opportunities for growth in this field. Platforms like Upwork, Fiverr, and Freelancer feature a wide range of consulting projects for freelancers with expertise in business strategies and operations.

In addition to general business consulting, professionals with legal expertise can expand their services globally by offering:

- Trademark and Copyright Advice
- DMCA Support
- Patent Research
- Brand Protection Services

These services are in high demand internationally, particularly with the increasing need for intellectual property protection and compliance in the global marketplace. Legal professionals can leverage their specialized knowledge to provide valuable guidance to startups, established businesses, and individuals across various industries.

Freelancers from diverse backgrounds can also explore niches such as startup consulting, crisis management, or funding strategy, allowing them to cater to businesses worldwide. By building strong profiles and staying updated on industry trends, freelancers can tap into the immense potential of this growing market.

Freelancing – In Search Of Halal Income

 Sven P. Taiwan
 Transformative Integrator - Operations & Project Management Specialist

$100/hr   100% Job Success $400K+ earned

One freelancer on Upwork charges $100 per hour for consulting services and has earned over $400,000 USD. [13] This demonstrates the significant earning potential in this field for those with expertise and dedication.

Ethical Considerations in Business Consulting

Although the risk of haram income in business consulting is lower than in some other fields, it is not completely absent. As a Muslim, it is essential to:

- Do not provide services to companies involved in unethical or prohibited activities such as gambling, interest-based financial services, or selling haram products.
- Do not fabricate data or share misleading insights that could harm a client's business.

Integrity is the foundation of a successful consulting career. By maintaining honesty and ethical practices, you can ensure that your income is halal and your work is pleasing to Allah.

Success Tips for Aspiring Business Consultants

To excel as a business consultant, you need focus, dedication, and the right strategies. Here's how you can build a successful career in this field:

- Don't rush after quick income. Take time to sharpen your skills and deepen your knowledge. Learn the tools and techniques essential for consulting, like project management tools, financial planning software, or market analysis frameworks. Stay updated with industry trends to provide relevant advice.
- Your profile is your first impression. Create a professional profile on platforms like Upwork, LinkedIn, or Fiverr. Highlight your expertise, key achievements, and successful projects. Use clear and concise

---

[13] https://www.upwork.com/freelancers/svenplisnier

- language to show your strengths. Include testimonials or feedback from past clients to build trust.
- Use platforms like LinkedIn to connect with business owners, CEOs, and HR managers. Engage in meaningful conversations, share your insights, and showcase your expertise through posts or comments. Strong connections can lead to long-term projects and repeat clients.
- Pick an area you enjoy and become an expert in it. For example, focus on startup consulting, financial analysis, or crisis management. Specialization helps you stand out in a competitive market and attract clients who value your unique expertise.
- Always provide honest advice and actionable insights. Avoid exaggerating results or misleading clients. Building trust through transparency ensures lasting relationships and repeat business.
- Use tools like Trello, Asana, or Notion to manage your projects and tasks. Keep track of client requirements, deadlines, and deliverables. Good organization shows professionalism and helps you deliver on time.
- The business world is always evolving so, read industry blogs, attend webinars, or take online courses to stay ahead. The more you learn, the better you can serve your clients.
- Success doesn't happen overnight. Start small and focus on delivering quality work. Consistency builds your reputation over time. Keep improving, and eventually, you'll establish yourself as a trusted consultant.

By following these steps, you can grow steadily in the consulting world. Success will come naturally when you focus on adding value and maintaining integrity in your work.

Business consulting is a field with immense potential for growth and income. With intelligence, hard work, and sincerity, you can achieve significant success, Insha'Allah. However, always remember to prioritize ethical practices and avoid haram activities in your work.

Instead of focusing solely on income, dedicate yourself to building your skills and knowledge. With Allah's blessings and your commitment to integrity, you'll find that halal income will come naturally, ensuring both professional and spiritual satisfaction.

Amazon Kindle / Self Publishing

Publishing a book traditionally often requires contacting various publishers, submitting your manuscript, and dealing with delays, especially for new authors. Due to not being widely popular, new writers often receive very low profit margins, making the whole process quite complicated.

However, this can be done much more easily through the Amazon platform. Amazon offers an option called KDP (Kindle Direct Publishing), which allows anyone to publish their book with ease. No help from a publisher is necessary. This method is known as Self Publishing. It's a fantastic business or freelance opportunity where you can sell your books worldwide through Amazon. For each sale, Amazon pays you a commission, and you set the price of your book, minus printing costs.

You can create and sell books on any topic you have knowledge of, and you don't need to be a poet or a literary writer. Many people worldwide are already using Amazon's self-publishing platform. Some even hire professional writers to create books and sell them on Amazon. However, it's important to note that you cannot publish books that infringe on someone else's copyright, and you must maintain proper quality standards. Failure to do so may result in your account being permanently banned by Amazon, preventing you from publishing any books.

Many people globally are using KDP to publish books. Most of them work on low-content books, such as journals, coloring books, sketchbooks, and activity books. These are easier to create compared to literary books. However, they do require design skills, as these books are design-dependent. To increase book sales, the cover page should have an attractive design. You can learn how to design book covers and interiors using Canva by following tutorials on YouTube.

Starting Your Own Book Business Easily

While writing and publishing books traditionally can be challenging, with **KDP**, you can start a business with low-content books. If you notice, children's books generally have very little content. They are often created with just a few graphics and minimal text. If you have design skills, you can create and publish these books yourself. Alternatively, you can hire a designer through freelance

Freelancing – In Search Of Halal Income

marketplaces to help you.

When working with children's books, it's important to note that you cannot use certain images or graphics, especially those of animals or other prohibited content.

Once you've designed a book—either on your own or with help from someone else—you need to create an account on kdp.amazon.com to sell it. After setting up your account, you can publish Kindle eBooks, Paperback, or Hardcover books.

You'll need to fill in the book's title, subtitle, author name, description, upload the book cover, and a copy of the book. Then, you can set your preferred price. Amazon will review your book, and once it's live, you will earn a commission whenever it sells. You can set the price however you like. Amazon will print and ship even a single copy directly to the customer. Payments for your book sales can be transferred to your local bank account.

Here following 50 low content book ideas:

Book Idea	Details of the Idea
Gratitude Journal	A list related to gratitude.
Dream Journal	A space to write down dreams and their interpretations.
Daily Planner	A planner for daily tasks, goals, and schedules.
Fitness Tracker	Track exercise, food, and progress.
Bullet Journal	Dot-grid pages for personal organization.
Expense Tracker	Record daily expenses and budgets.
Reading Log	Track books read, thoughts, and reviews.
Travel Log	Record dates, locations, and experiences.
Password Logbook	A place to securely store passwords.
Gardening Log	Track planting times, growth, and garden progress.
Adult Coloring Book	A coloring book with designs to relieve stress.
Children's Coloring Book	A coloring book for kids.
Mandala Coloring Book	A book for coloring Mandala designs.
Sudoku Puzzles	Various types of puzzle games.
Word Search Puzzles	Word search puzzle book.
Crossword Puzzles	Crossword puzzle book.
Maze Puzzles	Maze puzzle book.
Dot-to-Dot	A dot connection game for kids and adults.
Blank Recipe Book	A place to write favorite recipes.

Sketchbook	Blank pages for sketching.
Graph Paper Notebook	For math or design work.
Lined Notebook	Pages with lines for writing.
Travel Journal	A journal for travel-related notes and experiences.
Pregnancy Journal	Track each stage of pregnancy.
Prayer Journal	A journal for daily prayers.
Goal Setting Journal	Track and set personal goals.
Kids' Activity Journal	A creative activity journal for children.
Wedding Planner	A planner for all wedding-related details.
Meal Planner	Plan meals and grocery lists.
Project Planner	Track project deadlines and tasks.
Social Media Planner	Plan and track social media posts.
Blog Planner	Plan blog ideas and content.
Mood Tracker	Track mood patterns over time.
Pet Care Log	Track pet care routines and vet visits.
Mileage Logbook	Record vehicle mileage.
Workout Log	Record exercise and fitness progress.
Sketch and Doodle Book	A place for freehand drawing and doodling.
Quotes Journal	A journal for writing down favorite quotes.
Daily Affirmations Journal	Write down daily positive affirmations.
Language Learning Notebook	Practice and track new language learning.
Recipe Ingredients Notebook	Track ingredients for recipes.
Event Planning Book	Plan events and gatherings.
Nature Journal	Record observations and notes on nature.
Craft Project Notebook	Plan and track craft projects.
Buying Guide	Reviews and buying lists for various products.
Freelancing Journal	Track freelance work and progress.
Kids Grammar Book	A grammar book for kids.
Kids Math Book	A math book for kids.
Kids Word Book	A word learning book for kids.
ABC Tracing Workbook	A workbook to help kids practice handwriting.

If you create books based on the niches or topics mentioned above, while adhering to Sharia guidelines, you can earn halal income through KDP (Kindle Direct Publishing). The key to earning halal income from KDP lies in ensuring that the content of your books, as well as the overall business model, aligns with Islamic principles. This means avoiding any prohibited (haram) elements such as promoting immoral content, engaging in deceptive practices, or using copyrighted material without permission.

For instance, if you are creating activity books or journals, ensure that the content is constructive, educational, and family-friendly. If you are designing a children's book, make sure the themes and graphics are appropriate and do not involve anything that contradicts Islamic values, such as images of nude figures or depictions of violence. Similarly, when designing coloring books or puzzle books, focus on content that encourages learning, creativity, and positive engagement rather than promoting harmful or unethical behavior.

Furthermore, it's important to ensure that the book's cover design is attractive yet respectful, and you provide clear, honest descriptions of your books to potential buyers. By focusing on quality, ethical standards, and following Islamic guidelines, you can build a reputable and successful self-publishing business on Amazon.

KDP offers a global platform, so your books can reach a wide audience from various countries. The best part is that you maintain full control over your pricing, royalty, and distribution. As long as you stay true to Islamic principles and ensure that your books contribute positively to the readers, you can build a profitable, Sharia-compliant business that provides a halal source of income.

By focusing on providing value, maintaining integrity, and staying within the boundaries of what is permissible in Islam, you can make the most of this lucrative opportunity while staying true to your faith. Insha'Allah, your dedication and commitment to halal business practices will lead to success in your publishing endeavors.

Print on Demand

Print on Demand (POD) is a business model that allows designers to create and sell custom products online. Unlike traditional inventory-based models, POD eliminates the need for stock management. When a customer places an order, the design is printed on the product, and the product is then shipped directly to the customer. This business model is highly popular among graphic designers, illustrators, and artists who want to monetize their designs without worrying about production and shipping logistics. Two popular websites for the print-on-demand business with T-shirts are teespring.com and merch.amazon.com.

The concept of such a business can be easily found through Google or YouTube, but one important aspect that needs special attention is how to conduct this business in a halal manner.

Types of Products in POD

POD can be used for a variety of products, including:

- **T-shirts**: Custom-designed T-shirts are the most popular POD items.
- **Mugs**: Personalized mugs with unique designs.
- **Jewelry**: Custom jewelry designs, such as bracelets or necklaces.
- **Books**: Authors or designers can sell printed books or custom notebooks.
- **Hoodies**: Personalized hoodies with unique graphics or slogans.
- **Home Decor**: Custom pillows, blankets, or wall art.
- **Accessories**: Items like bags, hats, and phone cases.

Each product can be customized with a design, which is printed or created only when a customer places an order. This reduces the risk for the seller, as there is no need for upfront investment in inventory.

Popular Print on Demand Platforms

Here are two of the most popular POD platforms for T-shirts and other products:

Teespring.com

Teespring is a widely used POD platform where users can create and sell custom products, including T-shirts, mugs, and phone cases. It provides an easy-to-use interface for designers to upload their designs and set up their storefronts. Teespring handles the production, shipping, and customer service, allowing the designer to focus on creating and marketing their designs.

Merch.Amazon.com

Merch by Amazon is another platform where designers can upload their artwork and sell T-shirts and other products. The best part of Merch by Amazon is the exposure it provides, as it is directly integrated with the Amazon marketplace. Designers can take advantage of Amazon's massive customer base to sell their designs, while Amazon takes care of fulfillment.

How Print on Demand Works

The process of Print on Demand is simple and involves the following steps:

Create Your Designs

Designers create custom artwork or graphics that can be used on various products like T-shirts, mugs, or posters. These designs can be made using graphic design software such as Adobe Illustrator, Photoshop, or even free tools like Canva.

Upload Designs to a POD Platform

Once the designs are ready, they are uploaded to a print-on-demand platform like Teespring or Merch by Amazon. The designer can select which products to offer and apply their design to those products.

Set Product Prices

After uploading the design, the designer sets the retail price for each product. The POD platform usually handles the pricing structure, where the designer earns a royalty or commission for each product sold.

Promote and Sell

After setting up the storefront, the designer promotes their products through social media, websites, or digital marketing campaigns. When a customer places an order, the platform prints the design on the selected product and ships it directly to the customer.

Receive Earnings

Freelancing – In Search Of Halal Income

The designer earns a commission on each sale. The payment is typically processed by the POD platform on a regular basis, such as monthly or quarterly.

Conducting POD Business in a Halal Manner

While Print on Demand is an appealing business model, it is essential to ensure that the business is conducted in a halal manner according to Islamic principles. Some important guidelines to consider include:

Compliance with Islamic Ethics

- Ensure that the designs do not contain any haram or inappropriate content, such as images of alcohol, gambling, nudity, or anything that promotes unethical behavior.
- Avoid promoting or using offensive slogans or designs that may contradict Islamic values.

Avoiding Deception (Tawarruq)

- The business model should be transparent. Both the price and product description must be clear to the customer.
- Ensure that the delivery times, product quality, and other terms are agreed upon beforehand, and there should be no hidden fees.

Fair Business Practices

- It is important that the customer is aware of return and refund policies. A clear understanding of product delivery times, shipping details, and any potential problems that may arise should be communicated upfront.
- Platforms that offer returns and refunds ensure fairness and avoid any exploitation or ambiguity.

Avoiding Un-Islamic Imagery

- In the context of marketing, be mindful not to use un-Islamic imagery such as pictures of women, alcohol, or anything else deemed inappropriate in Islamic culture.
- Use only modest and acceptable designs that align with Islamic values.

According to a fatwa given by Mufti Faisal bin Abdul Hamid Al-Mahmudi

(Canada), the print-on-demand business can be considered permissible if conducted under the Ba'ī Salam (بيع السلم) method and fulfilling certain conditions.

Shariah Conditions:

- The product to be sold must have its weight, measurements, or unit specified.
- The product must be clearly defined, such as the size, pattern/print, price, etc., for a T-shirt.
- The quality of the product must be clearly stated.
- The delivery date of the product must be specified.

For the print-on-demand method, if the platform you work on ensures there is no opportunity for the buyer to be deceived, especially if the manufacturer company offers a return and refund policy for any issues, then the transaction will be valid.

Since the actual product owner is clearly specified, for example, if someone buys a T-shirt from teespring.com, they are aware that teespring will deliver the product on a certain date, with the product details and price being specified, and they are informed of the return and refund policies. In this case, the designer receives a commission whenever a design sells, which is predetermined with the company. Therefore, such business practices are considered halal according to the fatwa.

In this type of business, the product designs are usually displayed on mockups for various purposes. It is essential to ensure that no un-Islamic elements are included in these mockups. For example, to increase sales, one should avoid using images of women or any modified images that differ from the main product. This applies not only to print-on-demand businesses but to all types of businesses. Many people post images of women models to sell T-shirts on Facebook, but this should be avoided.

Print-on-demand (POD) work offers flexibility in how it can be managed, allowing designers to choose from a variety of platforms to sell their designs. You can directly create and sell your custom products via established POD websites, such as Teespring, Printful, Redbubble, or Merch by Amazon. These platforms handle the printing, packaging, and shipping, leaving you to focus solely on creating appealing designs and promoting them.

In addition to selling products directly, designers can also leverage online marketplaces like Fiverr, Etsy, Upwork, or Creative Market to sell their designs. These platforms allow you to offer digital designs for T-shirts, mugs, posters, and other merchandise without dealing with production or fulfillment. By listing your custom designs as digital products, you can sell them to businesses or individuals who will then handle the printing and sales.

Graphic designers, illustrators, and artists typically perform this work, as it involves creating high-quality, visually engaging artwork. However, in today's digital age, AI tools have made the design process easier, faster, and more accessible. Tools like Canva, Adobe Illustrator, and CorelDRAW offer features that help create designs even for those with limited graphic design experience. Additionally, AI-driven design platforms such as Designhill, Placeit, and Looka help users generate designs by simply inputting keywords or preferences, making the process even more efficient. These tools provide a wide range of customizable templates, allowing users to quickly create designs for various products such as T-shirts, posters, and more.

AI technologies are also being used to automate certain parts of the design process, such as resizing images, adjusting layouts, and generating new color schemes. This enables designers to produce multiple variations of a product design quickly, making it easier to test different concepts and increase the chances of making sales.

Overall, the combination of print-on-demand platforms and AI tools offers endless opportunities for graphic designers and entrepreneurs to create and sell custom designs, regardless of their skill level. Whether you're looking to manage everything yourself or just provide designs to businesses, the POD business model is a scalable and flexible way to turn your creativity into a source of income.

Question and answer

While writing the book, I encountered several questions regarding freelancing from different people. In particular, those who faced challenges while learning on their own. I gathered some of these questions after speaking with them. I have tried my best to provide accurate answers to those questions, hoping that newcomers who want to learn will, InshaAllah, benefit from them.

How Can I Learn by Watching Video Tutorials?

Many people face challenges when trying to learn by watching videos on YouTube. Especially for beginners, there are several common issues they encounter. In this section, I aim to address these issues and provide solutions to help newcomers who want to learn effectively.

Choosing the Right Video

When you search for tutorials on YouTube, a lot of videos show up. One of the biggest challenges for beginners is deciding which video to watch and whose video to follow. The key here is to find a video that provides sufficient information and quality content. Not every instructor has the same teaching method, and you won't get all the information from a single video.

Some YouTubers prioritize increasing their video views rather than providing comprehensive content. Be cautious about misleading titles or videos that promise quick fixes. For instance, some videos stretch a concept that could be covered in 5 minutes to 10, 20, or even 30 minutes, wasting time for beginners.

To avoid this, look for instructors whose videos provide enough detail without unnecessary fluff. You may need to watch a few random videos to identify channels that consistently provide valuable content. Once you find such channels, subscribe to them so you can learn from them regularly. This will help you stay updated and continue learning in a structured manner.

Time and Patience

Learning through video tutorials can be a rewarding process, but it requires both time and patience. If you don't have enough time to dedicate to watching the videos or lack the patience to engage with the content, it can become a real challenge. Watching videos is not a quick fix; it is an ongoing process that demands focus and commitment.

Unlike reading a book or taking a written course, video tutorials often require you to follow along with the instructor in real-time, which can take longer. It's easy to feel frustrated or overwhelmed if you're not prepared to dedicate enough time for consistent learning. This is especially true for beginners who are learning a new skill or concept for the first time.

One of the key aspects of effective video learning is active engagement. You cannot simply watch the videos passively and expect to retain the information. It's essential to practice as you go. For example, if you're learning programming, you should try writing the code alongside the tutorial, not just watching the instructor. Similarly, if you're learning design, practice applying the techniques on your own projects as you follow along. This hands-on approach will help solidify the concepts and make them easier to recall and apply in the future.

It's also important to be patient with yourself. Some concepts may take longer to grasp than others, and it's perfectly normal to revisit videos or tutorials multiple times. Learning takes time, and rushing through the material without fully understanding it can hinder progress in the long run. Setting aside regular, dedicated time for learning and practicing, along with staying patient and persistent, is crucial to success in mastering new skills through video tutorials.

By being mindful of the time commitment and practicing patience, you can make the most of your video learning experience and set yourself up for success.

Dealing with Video Updates and Interface Changes

Another common issue is the discrepancy between what is shown in the tutorial and what appears on your screen. For example, if the instructor is teaching Facebook marketing, and you notice that your screen doesn't match what's being shown in the video, this may be due to a version update on the platform.

Before getting frustrated, check the upload date of the video. If the video is older, it is likely that Facebook (or any other website) has updated its interface, causing differences in the user interface. It's important to adapt to the latest version by understanding the concepts discussed in the video and applying them to the new interface.

This issue is also prevalent in programming tutorials. In such cases, you must ensure that the software version and plugins used in the tutorial are compatible with the version you're working with.

Learning Through Online Courses

Many people choose to enroll in online courses to learn new skills. However, some may feel hesitant about whether online learning can be effective. One thing to keep in mind is that, when you watch videos from an online course, it's helpful to supplement that learning with additional YouTube videos on the same topic.

If you feel like you didn't fully understand a specific concept from the online course, watching a few more videos on YouTube can help clarify your doubts. This will give you a better understanding and fill in the gaps from the course. Try to explore additional videos that discuss the same topics covered in your online course lectures. This will complement your learning and give you a deeper understanding.

In conclusion, by combining video tutorials, online courses, and supplementary resources from platforms like YouTube, you can enhance your learning experience. Just make sure to follow reliable sources, stay patient, and practice consistently. By doing so, you can learn and apply new skills efficiently and effectively.

What Kind of Computer Do You Need for Freelancing?

When it comes to freelancing, one common question that arises is, "What kind of computer do I need?" The answer to this question is not straightforward because the type of computer required depends on the kind of work you plan to do.

Freelancing is not just a single field—there are multiple sectors, each with different requirements. For example, a graphic designer will need a different configuration compared to a web developer, and a web developer will need something different from a content writer. Each sector requires different minimum computer specifications to effectively perform the tasks.

For Graphic Design

If you're aiming to work in graphic design, you'll need a computer with a dedicated graphics card to handle design software like Adobe Photoshop, Illustrator, or other design tools. The computer should also have a high-quality processor to run these programs smoothly.

For the monitor, it's important to choose one with a 21-inch or larger screen and a 1920x1080 (Full HD) resolution for clearer visuals, especially when working with intricate designs. If you're on a budget, you can choose a monitor from any brand, as long as it meets these specifications.

For Web Development

Web developers need to run a variety of applications simultaneously, such as code editors, browsers, and server-side tools. A good processor, adequate RAM, and fast storage (like an SSD) are essential. While a graphics card is not as important for web development, having enough RAM and a fast SSD will ensure that everything runs efficiently and quickly, especially when managing multiple tasks at once.

3. For SEO Experts

SEO experts often work with several browser tabs open, analyze multiple websites, and perform multitasking. As a result, a computer with more RAM is beneficial to handle this level of multitasking. Additionally, a Solid State Drive

(SSD) is important for quicker data access, enabling faster website visits and efficient task execution.

4. For Content Writers

A content writer doesn't require a high-end computer with a dedicated graphics card or a powerful processor. A basic laptop or desktop with decent RAM (4GB or higher) and a good keyboard will suffice for writing tasks. However, if you plan to use heavy applications for editing and formatting, consider a better configuration with more RAM.

How to Choose the Right Computer for Your Budget

If you're just starting out with freelancing, let me tell you something—there's no need to go broke buying an expensive computer right off the bat. Trust me, your laptop from 2010 will work just fine for now. In fact, starting with a budget-friendly option is a brilliant move. The key is to focus on getting the **best configuration within your budget** for the kind of work you want to learn. The reality is, you don't need a $2,000 gaming PC to write blog posts, design a few logos, or manage your freelance accounts. Keep your wallet intact and your dreams big!

I'll give you a little peek into my past: back in 2009, when I was a fresh newbie in the freelancing world, I bought my first computer for **17,000 BDT** (or about **$170**). Honestly, that thing could barely handle a few tabs open, but I made it work. I was so proud of it—nothing like the feeling of spending your hard-earned money on a machine that could freeze up every 10 minutes! But I kept pushing forward, learning, and eventually, after some decent gigs, I upgraded to a laptop. Fast forward a few years, and with my own savings (and a lot of ramen noodles to survive), I finally got a high-end desktop. It was like going from a tricycle to a Ferrari, but it didn't happen overnight.

Now, here's the thing: don't go begging your parents to buy you the latest, super-powered computer just to impress your friends on social media. Trust me, I've seen plenty of people guilt-trip their parents into buying a $3,000 machine, only for them to give up on freelancing a month later. What happens? They end up with a shiny, expensive machine, but no clients to pay for it. So, here's the secret: buy a computer that fits your budget, start learning, and **get good** at freelancing first. Once you start making some serious money, then you can upgrade to that dream machine—no more freezing or crashing during important Zoom calls.

And remember, Rome wasn't built in a day, and neither will your perfect workstation. Start small, dream big, and once you've earned enough, you'll be upgrading to that high-end beast without breaking a sweat. You'll be sipping your coffee, laughing at your old computer, and thinking, "Wow, I really made it." Until then, your old trusty device will do just fine.

Finding the Right Configuration

To better understand computer configurations, there are many helpful YouTube channels that provide detailed reviews and build guides. One such popular channel is **Linus Tech Tips** (https://youtube.com/@LinusTechTips). You can visit their channel and check out their PC build guides in the playlist to help you make an informed decision about the computer that fits your needs and budget.

In conclusion, remember that the right computer for freelancing depends on the type of work you will be doing. Start with what you can afford, focus on learning, and gradually upgrade your equipment as your freelancing career progresses.

Laptop or Desktop: Which One is Better?

When it comes to buying a computer, one question that often leaves us in a dilemma is whether to buy a laptop or a desktop. Both types of computers have their own set of advantages and disadvantages.

For example, the laptop is highly portable, requires very little space to operate, and comes with a built-in screen, meaning you don't need a separate monitor. Additionally, the laptop's battery allows you to use it even when there's no electricity. On the other hand, a desktop has its own advantages, such as being easily upgradeable. Since it can be upgraded, a desktop can last much longer. Additionally, desktops are generally cheaper when compared to laptops with similar configurations.

Now, if your work requires you to travel to different places, carrying a desktop with you can be quite difficult. In contrast, a laptop is easy to carry and can be taken anywhere in your bag. Furthermore, in many areas, especially rural ones, power outages are common. In such places, desktops often fail to run smoothly due to frequent power cuts. In this case, a laptop is practically the only option. However, if you are planning to work on heavy tasks like video editing, graphic design, 3D modeling, motion design, etc., doing such tasks smoothly on a laptop may be challenging. For work like official tasks, web design, development, content writing, digital marketing, SEO, and affiliate marketing, a laptop will suffice.

Laptop vs. Desktop

Feature	Laptop	Desktop
Portability	Highly portable, easy to carry anywhere.	Not portable, fixed in one location.
Space Requirement	Minimal space required, no need for a separate monitor.	Requires a dedicated workspace and separate components.
Performance	Limited by compact hardware, though high-end models can handle demanding tasks.	Superior performance, especially for heavy tasks.
Upgradability	Limited; upgrades often	Easily upgradable,

	restricted to storage and RAM.	including CPU, GPU, and other parts.
Cost	Generally more expensive for equivalent configurations.	More cost-effective for the same performance level.
Power Backup	Built-in battery allows usage during power outages.	Requires continuous power; stops working during outages.
Durability	Breakdowns often require professional servicing.	Easier to repair or replace parts independently.
Suitability for Tasks	Ideal for light to moderate tasks (web design, content writing, SEO, etc.).	Best for heavy tasks (video editing, 3D modeling, etc.).
Lifespan	Limited due to compact, non-upgradable components.	Longer lifespan due to upgradability.

Some may argue, "I can do heavy tasks on my laptop," and yes, this depends on the laptop's configuration. Today, there are high-end laptops available that can handle demanding tasks, and if you can afford them, you will be able to do everything on a laptop. It will just cost you a bit more, that's all.

Personally, if someone asks me which device they should buy, I would recommend a desktop, provided there are no issues using one at home. When you set up a desktop in a specific place for work, it feels like you're really serious about your work. But working on a laptop while lying on the bed doesn't really create a productive environment. Additionally, desktops tend to break down less often, and many minor problems can be fixed on your own. With laptops, you often have to rush to a service center. Also, desktops can be easily upgraded as needed, which is another advantage. That's why I always suggest desktops for work.

Consider the type of work you'll do before choosing between a laptop or desktop. For tasks like graphic design or video editing, a desktop is better. If you move frequently or face power outages, a laptop is more practical.Ultimately, the decision is personal. Choose the device that best suits your needs and preferences for freelancing.

Freelancing – In Search Of Halal Income

Can I Freelance Without an NID?

Normally, NID (National Identity Card) is not issued to anyone under the age of 18. Even after turning 18, some people face delays in receiving their physical NID. As a result, many freelancers face difficulties when creating accounts on freelancing marketplaces. I've seen many cases where people create accounts under their parents' or relatives' names to start freelancing. While this might not cause immediate problems, it's not a good long-term strategy.

It's important to understand that your profile on a freelancing platform is essentially your portfolio, and this portfolio should ideally be in your own name. For instance, if you create an account under your mother's name, you'll have to use her picture as the profile photo. This not only goes against the principle of maintaining privacy but also could raise ethical concerns, as you're using someone else's identity. If clients find out that you're not using your real identity, they may develop a negative perception of you.

Moreover, if a client asks you to join a video call and realizes that the identity you've used is fake, it could lead to trust issues and affect your reputation.

Therefore, my advice is to use your real identity when creating an account on freelancing platforms. If you don't have an NID yet, it's better to wait and make efforts to get one rather than using someone else's information.

Risks of Using a False Identity

- If a client requests a video call and discovers that you're not the person represented on your profile, it could lead to immediate trust issues. This may harm your reputation and even result in the termination of your account.
- Misusing someone else's identity is a form of deceit. Clients value honesty, and if they suspect dishonesty, it can negatively impact their perception of you.
- Freelancing platforms often require identity verification, especially when withdrawing funds. Using a false identity can lead to complications during the verification process and may result in your account being suspended.

Some freelancers, particularly on platforms like Fiverr, use women's photos as profile pictures, thinking it might help them get more work. This is completely inappropriate. It is always best to work using your own identity on freelancing platforms. Trust that Allah will provide the sustenance that is meant for you. Trying to use deceptive methods, like using a woman's photo to attract more jobs, is misguided and wrong.

For men who don't have an NID, I recommend waiting until you receive your NID. Freelancing platforms allow you to create accounts, but your profile should always represent your personal identity. Using someone else's name or identity is not appropriate.

However, for women who don't have an NID, it's possible to use the ID of a male relative to create an account, provided that the intention is not to deceive. If you wish to maintain privacy or avoid showing your photo due to cultural reasons, this approach can work, but deception should never be part of the plan. Also, some women may try to present themselves provocatively on freelancing platforms to attract more clients. This is not permissible and should be avoided.

In summary always create your freelancing accounts with your real name and identity. Deception, whether for personal gain or privacy, can harm your credibility, reputation, and long-term success. Trust in Allah's provisions and focus on developing your skills and professionalism. By adhering to honesty and ethical practices, you'll build a career that is both successful and pleasing to Allah.

Which Skill Should I Learn?

This is a very common question, and I often find myself facing it. Many people, especially those starting out, want to know which skill they should focus on learning. The answer to this question is quite clear—it depends on you. Every person has their own creativity, preferences, and areas of interest. What may seem easy and enjoyable to me may not necessarily feel the same for you.

So, when you start learning a new skill, the first thing you must do is decide what interests you. You have the freedom to choose what to pursue. If you get caught up in too much indecision, learning may become difficult and overwhelming.

To truly master a skill, you can excel in almost any sector. For example, if you decide to learn web development, start by exploring tutorials and gaining a solid understanding of the field. Once you know what web development entails, then decide if it's the right choice for you. The same applies to other sectors as well. Each sector has its own market demand, and what's important is how much you can increase your own demand for that skill.

Looking ahead, fields like artificial intelligence, virtual reality, blockchain, and robotics are expected to grow significantly. You can certainly consider including these fields in your learning journey.

Another good approach is to explore freelance job listings on marketplaces. See what kinds of jobs are posted regularly, the rates offered, and how competitive the bidding process is. Researching these can give you a clear idea of what clients are looking for, and the competition you'll face in each area.

By observing profiles of freelancers who are already working in these areas, you can get insights into the types of jobs that are popular and successful. Take note of how they present their skills, the services they offer, and the reviews they receive. This can help you understand the qualities clients appreciate and the skill sets that bring the most success.

Personally, I've seen freelancers on marketplaces earning thousands of dollars working solely with basic tools like Microsoft Word and Microsoft PowerPoint. Each person works according to their own skill set and expertise. So, by analyzing these marketplace jobs, you'll get a good sense of which categories and skills are in demand. This proves that even simple skills, when mastered,

Freelancing – In Search Of Halal Income

can open doors to lucrative opportunities.

It's also worth mentioning that freelancing doesn't always require the most advanced or technical skills. Sometimes, soft skills like communication, organization, and time management can set you apart from competitors. Clients value reliability and professionalism as much as technical ability. Combining these traits with your chosen skill will make you a stronger candidate for any job.

Ultimately, the best skill to learn is the one you enjoy and are passionate about. If you focus on that and dedicate your time to mastering it, you will eventually become a successful freelancer, InshaAllah. Rather than chasing trends or trying to emulate others, build a foundation on what resonates with you.

There's no need to stress over seeing screenshots of others earning thousands of dollars. Focus on your own strengths and choose what you enjoy. If you learn the right way and with sincerity, Allah will grant you blessings in abundance. Remember, success is not just about earning money; it's about growing your skills, building confidence, and working in a way that aligns with your values and interests.

Can I Freelance Without Being Fluent in English?

This is a common question that many people ask, and you'll likely get two contrasting answers. Some will say that you don't need to know much English to freelance, while others will tell you that freelancing is impossible without knowing English. Interestingly, both answers can be correct, depending on the context.

The freelancer who says English isn't very important is likely referring to their own field, where English is not heavily required, or they may be managing with the level of English they know. As we've seen before, freelancing has many different sectors, and not all of them require advanced English skills.

On the other hand, the person who says you can't freelance without English is likely referring to their own experience. If they work with international clients or in fields like article writing, English is essential for communication and understanding the tasks.

Ultimately, it depends on the kind of work you're doing and who you're working for. Some sectors, like article writing, demand proficiency in English. If you're working with clients from other countries, you'll need English to communicate. However, formal grammar is not always necessary in these cases—many clients may also use tools like Google Translate, especially if they don't speak English fluently. So, there's no need to stress too much about perfect English.

However, keep in mind that English does open up a broader range of opportunities, especially since many clients on freelancing platforms use it for communication. You won't necessarily need to be fluent, but learning English will definitely add value to your skill set and help you succeed in the long run.

How to Learn English for Freelancing

If you want to improve your English, I recommend focusing on vocabulary first. Even if your grammar is good, a limited vocabulary will prevent you from expressing yourself clearly. So, try to learn new words every day.

Some people suggest watching English movies to learn the language, but I don't recommend this. Watching movies often leads to distractions and can sometimes pull you into inappropriate or haram content. Instead, focus on building your vocabulary and studying grammar to form sentences correctly.

You can join Facebook groups or language learning communities where you can practice speaking English with others. Don't worry about making mistakes—just keep practicing. You may face some teasing at first, but it's important not to stop speaking.

Reading English books or newspapers is also a great way to expand your vocabulary. When you encounter new words, look them up in a dictionary or on Google Translate, and try to memorize them. Keep a notebook where you can write down new words, and review them weekly.

Remember, you didn't learn to speak Bengali in just one or two days. It took years of practice and exposure. The same goes for English. Start small, learn words, then build sentences, and practice daily until you feel comfortable.

AI Tools for Learning English

Learning English requires consistent practice, and if you don't have people around you to practice with, there are plenty of apps and AI tools that can help you improve. Pi.ai is a great app where you can practice English with a virtual robot. This interactive platform allows you to hold conversations in English, helping you build confidence and improve your language skills.

Duolingo is another excellent app for learning languages, offering lessons that are both fun and engaging. It covers everything from vocabulary to grammar, and its gamified approach keeps you motivated as you track your progress.

To work on pronunciation, Elsa Speak is a great option. This app uses AI to help you refine your pronunciation, providing instant feedback so you can sound more natural. You can also use Google Translate for quick translations and to hear how words are pronounced, which is helpful for beginners.

AI tools like ChatGPT can also be invaluable for language practice. You can type or speak in English, and ChatGPT will respond, helping you practice sentence formation, expand your vocabulary, and even improve your pronunciation through voice features. If you have specific questions about English grammar, pronunciation, or word usage, you can get immediate assistance, making it a useful resource for quick clarifications.

While fluency in English is certainly beneficial for freelancing, it's not a barrier to starting. With consistent practice using the right tools, you can improve your English over time and gain the confidence needed to excel in the freelancing world.

Which Job is Easier and Offers Higher Income?

When thinking about freelancing, one common question that comes to mind is: Which job is easier and offers more income? In my opinion, the relationship between the difficulty of a job and the income it generates is inversely proportional. In other words, the easier the job, the lower the pay, and the harder the job, the higher the pay. This is because jobs that are easier tend to have more competition, which drives the pay down, whereas harder jobs have fewer competitors and therefore higher pay.

Once you learn a difficult skill, it often doesn't feel as hard as it initially seemed. Many people may think a certain skill is challenging, but with regular practice, it becomes easier over time. A good analogy is the beautiful recitation of the Quran that captivates us. Initially, learning to recite may seem difficult, but with continuous practice, it becomes much easier, and those who persist can even become Hafiz of the Quran.

No one can tell you for sure which field will bring you the most money. The answer depends on your individual skills, experience, and even your fate. A highly skilled person may not succeed if it's not meant for them, while someone with fewer skills may find success due to their fate. Believing in your Qadr (fate) is essential, as it's a fundamental part of faith.

Fields like Search Engine Optimization (SEO), Digital Marketing, Brand Promotion, and Affiliate Marketing may seem easier for some people compared to other jobs. In the context of freelancing, I've tried to highlight areas where you can earn halal income. Alhamdulillah, Allah grants blessings in halal earnings. Therefore, rather than chasing higher income, it's wiser to seek barakah (blessing) in your earnings. Barakah is essential in all areas of life. Without barakah, even abundant wealth can lead to stress and worry. This is why the Prophet (PBUH) always prayed for barakah, not just for himself but also for others.

In conclusion, focus on the skill that aligns with your strengths and interests. Keep faith in your abilities and your fate, and prioritize seeking barakah in your work. With sincerity, dedication, and halal earnings, you'll find both success and peace.

How to Learn Freelancing from Home?

Many people, when thinking about learning freelancing, initially look for training centers. I often receive messages asking for recommendations on which training center to choose. My answer is usually the same: start by watching subject-specific tutorials on YouTube, practice, and learn on your own.

For example, if you want to learn web development but aren't sure what exactly to study or what to search for, it can be tricky in the beginning. Here's a helpful formula that I use:

First, search Google to create a list of training centers offering web development courses. Visit their websites or check their Facebook pages for course details. Collect information on what modules or curriculum they offer in these courses. For instance, if you gather course plans from five different centers, you will have a good idea of what to learn. Now, using this information, search for tutorials on YouTube or Google related to these topics. Learn and practice as you go.

Although this approach might take longer, you'll gain a thorough understanding of the topic. Unlike a training center where you might learn a specific lesson in a short amount of time, searching and watching YouTube videos gives you access to multiple instructors and perspectives on the same topic. You can learn different solutions and approaches to the same problem without spending money on a training center. It's a cost-effective way to learn from the comfort of your home.

However, some people find it difficult to learn just by watching videos and doing independent research. While watching a tutorial, you may encounter questions or parts you don't understand. In such cases, a mentor can be extremely helpful. You can definitely learn on your own, but it will take more time and effort.

If you prefer learning from training centers, you can definitely collect course modules as mentioned above and follow that process. But keep in mind, many people struggle with this method because it can take a lot of time, and the constant search for information can lead to frustration, causing them to lose interest. Additionally, misleading video titles or incomplete tutorials might force you to watch several videos to get the full picture.

Another challenge is that some may have limited basic computer skills, making it harder to understand certain videos. My advice is to start by improving your basic computer skills.

Before diving into advanced freelancing topics, focus on improving your basic computer skills. Understanding file management, typing, and using essential tools like Microsoft Office will make learning more technical skills easier.

Once you have gained the basic knowledge, you can move on to advanced topics and learn them from home, without needing to attend a physical training center.

Tips for Staying Motivated

- Define what you want to achieve and break it down into manageable milestones.
- Dedicate a specific time each day to learning and practicing.
- Join online forums or social media groups where learners share tips, solve problems, and exchange resources.
- The more you apply what you've learned, the faster you'll develop confidence and expertise.

Learning freelancing from home requires determination, patience, and consistent effort. While it may take longer than enrolling in a training center, the rewards are worth it. You'll not only gain skills but also learn how to solve problems independently—a crucial trait for any freelancer.

By leveraging free resources, seeking mentorship when needed, and staying focused, you can successfully build your freelancing career from the comfort of your home. If you need any help or suggestions feel free to email me at mdnurullah80@gmail.com

How to Bid and Secure Jobs Easily?

There is no fixed rule for writing a cover letter, but when you bid for a job on freelancing marketplaces, submitting a well-written cover letter or proposal can increase your chances of getting hired. Many freelancers fall into the trap of copying and pasting the same cover letter repeatedly, which is a mistake. Doing this may result in account suspension, and more importantly, it will lead to frustration from not landing any work.

When a client posts a job, they are not expecting a generic cover letter. If you read the job description carefully, ask relevant questions, and share your experience with similar tasks, you increase your chances of getting hired.

Here are some tips to help you create an effective cover letter:

- Take the time to carefully read and re-read the job posting. Understand exactly what the client is looking for, including their goals, expectations, and any specific requirements. This ensures your response is aligned with their needs.
- Instead of starting with "Hi," "Hello," or "Dear Sir," grab the client's attention by addressing the specifics of the job. For example, begin with something like, "I noticed your need for a skilled [role] to handle [specific task]." This shows you are focused on their project from the start.
- Always mention your previous experience with similar projects. However, there's no need to flood the client with too many links. Instead, explain how you plan to tackle the project, outlining your process clearly. This shows that you have a well-thought-out plan for completing the work.
- If the job posting includes specific questions, address them directly and confidently in your proposal. Avoid uncertain phrases like "Maybe I can do that." Instead, use clear, assertive language like, "Yes, I can complete this task effectively." Confidence builds trust and increases the likelihood of being hired.
- Ask relevant questions in your cover letter, but avoid making them seem like you lack confidence. For example, you could ask, "What is your timeline for completion?" or "Will the content be provided, or should I create it?" This shows you are engaged and thoughtful about the project.

- Try to keep your cover letter as concise as possible. Avoid adding unnecessary details, as long cover letters can overwhelm the client. If your cover letter is too lengthy, the client may skip it and move on to the next proposal.
- Avoid using a one-size-fits-all cover letter. Tailor each proposal to the specific job. Mention something unique about the client's project or business to show genuine interest.
- Include a brief overview of how you plan to tackle the project. For example, "To complete this task, I will begin by [specific step], then proceed to [next step], ensuring [desired outcome]." This demonstrates your understanding and strategic thinking.
- Avoid typos, grammatical errors, or overly casual language. A polished and professional tone builds credibility and reflects your attention to detail.
- Conclude your proposal by inviting the client to discuss further. For example, "I'd be happy to discuss your project in more detail and answer any additional questions you might have. Looking forward to working with you!"

By following these tips and personalizing your cover letter to each job, you will increase your chances of getting hired. Always focus on the job's requirements and be relevant in your responses. Avoid irrelevant details or too many links, and make sure your proposal is focused on the task at hand.

InshaAllah, if you consistently follow this approach, landing jobs on freelancing marketplaces will become easier.

How to Receive Payment for Freelancing?

If you are working with international clients, it is recommended to do the work through a **freelancing marketplace**. This not only helps build your marketplace profile but also simplifies the payment process. Most marketplaces collect payment from the client before the work starts, and once the work is successfully completed, the marketplace transfers the payment to the freelancer's account. From there, you can withdraw the funds through your bank.

To ensure there are no issues during the process, make sure that the name on your marketplace account matches the name on your NID (National ID) or passport, and use the same name on your bank account. If you don't have a bank account, you can Mobile Banking Service to withdraw the payment. When using Bank, ensure to use the proper SWIFT code of your bank.

Currently, almost all freelancing marketplaces allow you to withdraw funds via bank transfers. If you prefer, you can use a MasterCard. A reliable provider of MasterCards for freelancers is Payoneer. By registering on Payoneer, you will receive an international MasterCard, which allows you to withdraw funds at any ATM that supports MasterCard in Bangladesh. Payoneer also provides a US bank account, where you can transfer dollars, which can then be withdrawn via Payoneer MasterCard at ATMs or through services like bKash or Ucash.

If you are working with clients outside the marketplace, one of the easiest ways to receive payments is through money transfer websites like Taptapsend, Riamoneytransfer, Wise, WorldRemit, Western Union, or Xoom. These services generally support business transactions, though some may require a business account. Be sure to read the terms and conditions of the money transfer website carefully to avoid complications.

For example, I have personally used Wise and Taptapsend many times, but with Wise, you must be careful. Wise does not allow currency exchange transactions, and the same applies to Payoneer. If you send dollars to someone without a valid reason, you may be questioned, and your account could be banned. So, avoid engaging in any illegal transactions.

Always remember: as long as you earn money online legally, there are many ways to bring the money into the country. The focus should initially be on how to earn halal income online, and you can worry about the payment method later.

Can I Freelance Using a Mobile Phone?

If you don't have a laptop, you can still do some freelancing tasks using your mobile phone. However, for professional and extensive work, a computer is indispensable. There are certain freelancing tasks that can be done in a limited way on mobile, such as:

- Content Writing
- Translation
- Copywriting
- Blog Commenting
- Forum Posting
- Virtual Assistant (to a limited extent)
- Proofreading
- Product Description Writing
- Transcription
- Online Tutoring

That being said, it's important to stay away from tempting apps that claim to help you earn money on your mobile. Most of these apps are designed to deceive people, and you won't be able to perform legitimate freelancing work on them.

If you must work on your mobile, choose quality tasks like article writing. This is a task that can be done both on a computer and a mobile device. However, working on a mobile may pose some challenges, such as difficulty with research and content formatting.

Nowadays, computers are much more affordable, and you can buy a desktop for around $100 – 150$. Websites like Bikroy.com and various Facebook groups have ads for these computers. If you choose to buy one, be sure to check the configuration carefully and meet the seller in person to avoid any scams. By doing so, you can ensure that you are not deceived.

When Should I Bid to Get a Job on a Marketplace?

There's no fixed time to bid that guarantees you'll get hired on a freelance marketplace, but timing your bids strategically can significantly increase your chances. Bidding immediately after a job is posted is often the best approach, as clients tend to receive numerous proposals quickly. Being one of the first to apply helps your bid stand out and increases the likelihood of it being reviewed.

Since many freelancing clients come from countries like the USA, the UK, or other Western nations, aligning your bidding times with their time zones is a smart strategy. Clients are typically more active during their daytime, which may coincide with late evening or nighttime in other regions. By bidding during these hours, you increase the chances of your proposal being seen when clients are actively searching for freelancers.

For example, if you know that a majority of clients are located in the USA, consider bidding during their business hours. Many job postings occur during this time, and being prompt ensures your bid is among the first they review. Additionally, clients often check bids early in the morning, so having your proposal ready before their day starts can give you a competitive edge.

Marketplaces That Don't Require Bidding

While many platforms operate on a bidding system, some marketplaces don't require freelancers to bid for jobs. Instead, you create a listing of your services, and clients come to you. Popular platforms with this model include:

- Fiverr.com
- Seoclerk.com
- Legiit.com

On these platforms, freelancers create gig listings showcasing their skills and services. Clients browse these listings and hire freelancers directly based on their needs. Recently, **Upwork** has introduced a similar feature called "Projects," where freelancers can list their services, allowing clients to hire them without the need for bidding.

Tips for Bidding Success

Be Prompt: Bidding immediately after a job is posted increases the chances of your proposal being seen.

Align with Client Time Zones: Research your target client's time zone and adjust your bidding schedule to match their active hours.

Personalize Your Proposal: Avoid sending generic bids. Tailor each proposal to the client's specific requirements to stand out.

Monitor High Activity Hours: Keep track of when new jobs are frequently posted and schedule your bidding accordingly.

By combining these strategies and leveraging marketplaces that fit your strengths, you can improve your chances of landing jobs and building a successful freelancing career. Whether through timely bidding or optimizing your service listings, understanding client behavior is key to success.

Why Can Freelance Marketplace Accounts Get Banned?

There are several reasons why a freelance marketplace account may get banned, and it's crucial for every freelancer to be aware of these to avoid losing their hard-earned profile. Once your account gets banned, it can be very difficult, if not impossible, to recover it. Therefore, before creating an account on any marketplace, make sure to thoroughly read their Terms of Service.

To avoid having your account banned, keep the following points in mind:

- When creating an account, make sure your name matches the name on your official documents, such as your national ID or passport. Mismatched or false information can raise suspicion and lead to account suspension. This is especially important when withdrawing funds, as payment providers often cross-check your details.
- Freelance marketplaces generally require freelancers to use their internal communication platforms. Sharing personal contact details such as phone numbers, emails, or Skype accounts is against their rules. Even sharing a portfolio website that includes contact information can be flagged as an attempt to bypass the marketplace, resulting in a ban. Always communicate and share work exclusively through the platform.
- Having more than one account on the same marketplace is strictly prohibited. Some freelancers create multiple accounts to secure more work, but this is considered a violation. Marketplaces monitor IP addresses, device usage, and account activities, so managing multiple accounts is likely to be detected and lead to a permanent ban. Stick to using a single account and focus on building it up.
- Sending mass messages or spam to clients or other freelancers can result in account suspension. This behavior is often seen as unprofessional and disruptive. Additionally, repeatedly bidding on jobs without success can also raise red flags. Marketplaces may interpret this as an indication of inadequate skills, which could lead to account restrictions or suspension.
- Buying fake reviews or asking clients for unwarranted reviews is strictly against marketplace policies. If detected, your account could face a permanent ban. Authentic reviews reflect genuine work quality and help build trust, so focus on earning honest feedback through your

work.
- Some freelancers use browser extensions or bots to keep their accounts online 24/7. This is a direct violation of most marketplaces' policies. Such behavior is unnatural, and marketplaces have algorithms that detect these patterns. Being online constantly without actual activity can lead to suspicion and eventually account suspension.
- Copying gig images, descriptions, or titles from other freelancers is not only unethical but also against platform rules. Plagiarized content damages your reputation and can result in account restrictions. Invest time in creating original gig descriptions, using your own words to showcase your skills and services.
- Similar to gig content, copying someone else's profile information, including their bio, skills, or experience, is prohibited. Your profile should uniquely reflect your own expertise and background. Plagiarism can lead to your account being flagged or banned.
- Each platform has specific rules regarding how freelancers and clients should communicate. For example, requesting payment outside the platform is strictly forbidden and is considered an attempt to bypass the marketplace's fees. Always adhere to these guidelines to avoid penalties.
- Being rude, unprofessional, or failing to deliver work as promised can result in negative feedback or disputes. Accumulating such issues could lead to account warnings or eventual suspension. Always prioritize clear communication and quality delivery.

Once your account is banned, it may be impossible to recover, so always follow the rules and work with caution to avoid violations and ensure uninterrupted success.

Tips for Long-Term Success on Freelance Marketplaces:

- Thoroughly read the **Terms of Service** for the platform you are using and ensure you understand their rules.
- Regularly update your profile and keep your information accurate and professional.
- Focus on building trust with clients by delivering high-quality work and communicating effectively.
- Be patient and work consistently to grow your reputation, as shortcuts or rule violations can jeopardize your account.

By following these guidelines, you can avoid potential pitfalls and build a sustainable freelancing career while maintaining the integrity of your account. Remember, one of the keys to success in freelancing is to operate with professionalism, honesty, and respect for the marketplace's rules.

What is the best guideline for learning web development?

The first step in learning web development is to master HTML and CSS. Once you have a solid grasp of these basics, the next step is to learn various front-end frameworks like Bootstrap, Tailwind CSS, and others. After that, you can move on to learning SASS, SCSS, and advanced CSS techniques.

Once you are comfortable with HTML and CSS, focus on learning JavaScript. If you want to specialize in front-end development, after mastering HTML and CSS, JavaScript should be your priority

Roadmap for Learning Web Development

HTML and CSS: Learn to structure web pages and style them using CSS.

- Build small projects like personal portfolios, landing pages, or blogs.

Responsive Design: Learn to create mobile-friendly designs using media queries and frameworks like **Bootstrap** or **Tailwind CSS**.

Advanced CSS: Dive into **SASS** and **SCSS**, and learn advanced techniques like grid layouts, animations, and transitions.

JavaScript Basics: Understand core concepts such as:

- Variables, data types, and functions.
- Conditions, loops, and arrays.
- Learn DOM Manipulation and Events:

APIs and JSON: Understand how to fetch and manipulate data using **AJAX** and APIs.

JavaScript Frameworks: Once comfortable with JavaScript, choose a framework based on your goals:

- **React**: Ideal for building dynamic, interactive user interfaces.
- **Vue.js**: Great for progressive web apps and lightweight projects.
- **Angular**: Suitable for full-stack applications.

Version Control: Learn **Git** and **GitHub** for collaboration and project management.

Back-End Development (Optional): If you're interested in full-stack development, learn:

- **Node.js** for server-side programming.
- **Databases** like MongoDB or MySQL.

Build Projects: Practice everything you've learned by creating real-world projects like:
To-do lists.

- Blog platforms.
- Weather apps using APIs.

Participate in Challenges: Enhance problem-solving skills on platforms like **LeetCode**, **HackerRank**, or **Codewars**.

My advice is to prioritize becoming proficient in JavaScript before diving into any frameworks. JavaScript is the foundation of modern web development, and a strong understanding of it will allow you to work with any JavaScript framework with ease. Once you're comfortable with the core concepts of JavaScript—such as variables, functions, loops, objects, and arrays—you'll have a solid base for learning more advanced topics like ES6+ features, asynchronous programming, and APIs.

After mastering the basics, you can move on to learning JavaScript frameworks. Each framework has its strengths, and knowing JavaScript deeply will make it easier to adapt to any of them. For instance, if you want to build dynamic, interactive user interfaces, learning React might be a good choice. On the other hand, if you're working with a full-stack application, Angular or Vue.js might be more appropriate.

Additionally, to further improve your skills, participate in coding challenges or contribute to open-source projects. Platforms like LeetCode, HackerRank, and Codewars offer various challenges that can help you refine your coding and problem-solving abilities. Working on these challenges will not only deepen your understanding of JavaScript but also sharpen your ability to write clean, efficient, and optimized code.

By gaining a deep understanding of JavaScript and regularly practicing through projects and coding challenges, you'll build the skills needed to succeed in any web development role. The more you practice and experiment, the more confident you'll become in working with JavaScript and its frameworks.

Is it Halal to Do Survey Work on Foreign Websites?

Typically, survey work on foreign websites, especially those using a VPN from the USA
or other developed countries, requires the creation of fake profiles. These profiles are used to make it appear as if the person taking the survey is a resident of that particular region, while in reality, the work is being done from elsewhere.

Moreover, the products for which feedback is collected in surveys are often not 100% halal. Frequently, feedback is requested for products like alcohol, cigarettes, and tobacco, which are prohibited in Islam. Even when there are halal products in surveys, giving false feedback without actually using the product is deceitful. This involves lying, trickery, and various forms of haram activities, making these tasks unacceptable in Islam.

Let's consider a simple example. Imagine I've developed an educational app designed to help high school students improve their study habits. My target customers are students from various schools and colleges in a specific region, let's say a city like Istanbul or a town in Texas. To ensure the app meets their needs, I decide to conduct a survey to gather opinions and feedback from students in that region.

To achieve this, I hire a company that specializes in conducting surveys among local students. However, instead of collecting genuine responses from students in Istanbul or Texas, the company fabricates the survey data or collects responses from individuals outside the target region who have no relevance to my product. They present this false data as authentic, and I unknowingly base my business decisions on it.

Now imagine the consequences. I might adjust my app's features or pricing based on this misleading feedback, only to find that my changes do not resonate with my actual audience. This could lead to poor sales, negative reviews, and significant financial losses. The harm isn't just monetary—it damages the trust between my business and my customers, all because of a foundation built on deceit.

Similarly, when individuals participate in online survey work under false pretenses, they engage in multiple layers of deception. For instance, someone might create fake profiles claiming to be from a specific region to qualify for surveys, despite having no connection to the target audience. This dishonesty misleads companies relying on the data, affecting their decisions and potentially causing harm to their businesses.

Islam strongly condemns such practices. Deceit and fraud go against the core principles of honesty and integrity that every Muslim is obligated to uphold. Providing false information, even for personal gain, not only undermines trust but also aligns with the traits of hypocrisy.

Engaging in deceitful practices for monetary gain is not just a moral failure but also a betrayal of Islamic values. Allah (SWT) warns us in the Quran:

"Among the people are those who say, 'We believe in Allah and in the Last Day,' but they are not believers. They try to deceive Allah and those who believe, but they only deceive themselves, and they do not perceive. In their hearts is a disease, and Allah has increased their disease, and for them is a painful punishment because they used to lie."

I had a friend who once called me and said he was doing survey-related work and wanted to buy a new computer so that his wife could do these tasks from home. He asked me if it was right to engage in survey work and what kind of computer he should buy. After discussing the matter, I advised him not to pursue survey work, even though he had spent money to buy an IP address for this purpose.

Many people on YouTube promote survey work, often to promote their referral links.

What they don't realize is that they are encouraging others to engage in haram activities, and the sin for that will also be recorded in their deeds. Therefore, we should always discourage bad practices and encourage good ones.

Allah (SWT) says:

"Help one another in righteousness and piety."

To those in Bangladesh engaging in survey work on foreign websites, my advice is to stop and instead focus on learning data entry and processing tasks, or other easier jobs. While survey work might earn you a small amount of money temporarily, it will not bring any long-term benefits to your career.

Instead of engaging in deceptive survey work, why not learn to work honorably by mastering tools like Microsoft Excel or PowerPoint, which will allow you to earn with dignity?

Will a Freelancer Work Late Nights Forever?

Many freelancers wonder whether they will have to work late into the night for the rest of their lives. The idea of working at night has become a trend for many people today. It's common to see people spending extra hours on their phones, scrolling through social media or watching YouTube videos, only to fall asleep at 2 or 3 AM. However, for an established freelancer, working late into the night is not necessary.

An experienced freelancer will typically have long-term clients and will communicate their working hours to them. This means they can deliver work according to their own schedule, without needing to work overnight. While it might be necessary to work late when starting out, it is important to gradually reduce late-night working hours.

For newcomers, my advice is to bid for jobs during the day. Try to start working early in the morning, right after Fajr (dawn) prayers. This will give you plenty of time during the day to complete your tasks.

Working late into the night for long periods can cause various health issues. While these may not be noticeable initially, over time, problems like high blood pressure, weight gain, and heart diseases may arise. The most important issue is that working late often interferes with timely prayers. It becomes difficult to perform Fajr and other prayers on time when you're up until 2 or 3 AM, making it harder to engage in worship.

We must remember that we were not created to be awake all night just for freelancing. Allah created the night for rest and recuperation. Our beloved Prophet Muhammad ﷺ disliked staying up late and would encourage the companions to go to sleep soon after Isha (night) prayer. Freelancing should not become a reason to stay awake all night and neglect this Sunnah.

7 Benefits of Sleeping Early:

1. Sleeping early reduces the risk of chronic conditions like heart disease, high blood pressure, and obesity.

2. A good night's sleep improves focus, memory, and cognitive performance, helping you work more effectively during the day.

3. Adequate sleep decreases stress and anxiety, promoting a more positive outlook on life.

4. Sleeping early strengthens your immune system, making you less prone to illnesses.

5. Waking up early after proper rest ensures you feel refreshed and energetic throughout the day.

6. Sleep regulates hormones that control appetite, stress, and overall well-being.

7. Early sleep makes it easier to wake up for Fajr and stay consistent in prayers, strengthening your spiritual health.

Personally, I used to work late into the night due to my lack of awareness. Once I learned about the importance of following the Sunnah, where our Prophet ﷺ advised going to sleep early, I decided to change my habits. I informed my clients of my working hours, and the results were positive. Gradually, waking up early became a routine for me. Alhamdulillah, with a little determination, I was able to adopt this practice. It's important to note that with sincere effort, we can develop positive habits, but without that effort, good habits are often difficult to establish.

In conclusion, freelancers should adopt balanced working hours that align with Islamic principles and promote a healthy lifestyle. Late nights might feel necessary at first, but they are not sustainable. By prioritizing early mornings, timely prayers, and proper rest, freelancers can achieve both professional success and spiritual well-being.

How Can Madrasa Students Freelance?

There was a time when madrasa students were often undervalued, seen as limited to religious roles. But times have changed. Today, madrasa students are making significant strides in competitive fields worldwide, securing positions in prestigious universities and institutions. This success is a testament to their dedication, intellectual abilities, and evolving educational environments. Parents no longer view madrasas as places only for children struggling academically. Instead, modern madrasas are transforming into centers of well-rounded education, combining religious teachings with essential subjects like English, Science, and Literature. These changes prepare students for success in both religious and secular careers.

A solid education paired with a strong foundation of faith is crucial for every student. Whether the curriculum is religious or secular, combining the two equips students with the tools they need to thrive in today's world. Madrasa students, with their unique skill set, can achieve just as much as their peers in regular schools and colleges. In fact, they hold a distinct advantage in freelancing, especially in areas like Arabic translation and content creation.

Platforms like Upwork and Fiverr offer a wealth of opportunities for madrasa students, particularly in Arabic translation. Jobs range from translating religious texts, documents, and articles to assisting businesses with bilingual communication needs. Many madrasa students already possess a high level of proficiency in Arabic, which gives them an edge in this competitive market. On Upwork, you'll find consistent demand for tasks like Arabic-to-English and English-to-Arabic translations. Similarly, on Fiverr, students can create gigs offering translation services and start building their freelancing portfolio.

Their deep understanding of Islamic terminology and cultural nuances allows madrasa students to excel in niches like Quranic translation, Islamic book editing, and developing educational materials for Islamic studies. Beyond translation, there are opportunities to teach Arabic online, create Arabic language tutorials, or write scholarly articles on Islamic topics.

For those with technical knowledge, freelancing can go even further. Students can write articles in Arabic, create and sell Arabic language learning resources like e-books, worksheets, or online courses, and even design apps or websites tailored to Arabic-speaking audiences. Arabic proofreading and editing services are also in high demand, particularly for academic papers, religious content, and

Freelancing – In Search Of Halal Income

legal documents.

With dedication and the right technical skills, madrasa students can create digital products or services that contribute positively to spreading Islamic knowledge while earning a halal income. The growing globalization of the job market has significantly increased the demand for skilled Arabic translators and content creators, making this a valuable opportunity for madrasa students to thrive.

By focusing on improving their skills, building a strong portfolio, and actively engaging in online freelancing communities, madrasa students can unlock these opportunities. This is more than just a way to earn money—it's a way to integrate faith and work, proving that success in the modern world can be achieved while staying true to Islamic principles

Writing & Translation > Translation

I will translate arabic to english, english to arabic translation, arabic translation

 exitooo Level 2 Seller | ★ ★ ★ ★ ★ 5 (952) | 9 Orders in Queue

For example, a freelancer from Egypt offers Arabic-to-English and English-to-Arabic translation services on Fiverr. As a Level 2 Seller, they charge $5 to $30 for translations ranging from 250 to 1500 words. Their delivery time ranges from 12 hours to 48 hours, and they currently have 9 pending orders. This shows how consistent work in this area can lead to a steady flow of income.

Basic	Standard	Premium
Advanced 48 hours		$30
1500 words from English to Arabic • OR • 1000 words from Arabic to English		

Beyond translation, their deep understanding of Islamic terminology and cultural nuances allows madrasa students to excel in niches like Quranic translation, Islamic book editing, and developing educational materials for

Islamic studies. There are also opportunities to teach Arabic online, create Arabic language tutorials, or write scholarly articles on Islamic topics.

For those with technical knowledge, freelancing can go even further. Students can write articles in Arabic, create and sell Arabic language learning resources like e-books, worksheets, or online courses, and even design apps or websites tailored to Arabic-speaking audiences. Arabic proofreading and editing services are also in high demand, particularly for academic papers, religious content, and legal documents.

On Fiverr, you'll also find gigs for Arabic article writing. If you're proficient in English, you can combine your skills and write articles in both languages. To start, create writing examples in both Arabic and English to showcase your talent.

To succeed in this field, study how to write SEO-friendly articles—there are many YouTube tutorials that can help improve your writing skills. Joining Facebook groups for writers and sharing your work will also aid your development. Regular writing practice and reading the work of others will significantly enhance your writing quality.

You can further build your portfolio by sharing your articles on platforms like Medium, Scoop.it, LinkedIn Articles, and SlideShare. Once you have a strong writing portfolio, pay attention to Facebook groups where writers are hired. Gaining experience in these groups can help you grow your confidence and prepare you to create accounts on freelancing marketplaces and actively bid for jobs.

In conclusion, freelancing is a fantastic opportunity for madrasa students, especially in areas like Arabic translation and article writing. By focusing on improving your skills, building a strong portfolio, and being proactive in online communities, you can easily start earning through freelancing while maintaining your religious principles.

Can Women Freelance While Maintaining Hijab?

Freelancing is often done from home, and many people tend to think of it as a job suited for women, as they spend much of their time at home. However, with the right Islamic environment, women can safely and securely engage in freelancing while maintaining their hijab and adhering to Islamic principles.

There are many fields in freelancing, such as web design and development, graphic design, digital marketing, content writing, and translation, that can easily be done from home. These professions, when done correctly, pose minimal risks and can be done safely, without compromising one's faith or modesty.

For example, many women work as designers, creating themes, plugins, or templates to sell on marketplaces, and they are earning well, Alhamdulillah. There are also many women content writers who work from home, producing articles or other content. Women who have studied English can easily excel in content writing.

It is crucial to remember that Islam strictly prohibits any involvement in activities that are deemed haram (forbidden). This includes working with content that promotes pornography, violence, or anything that goes against the ethical and moral guidelines of Islam. Freelancers, whether male, female, or non-binary, must be diligent in ensuring that the work they engage in aligns with the principles of Islam. Freelancing is an opportunity to work independently, but it also comes with the responsibility of maintaining integrity and upholding Islamic values.

As a freelancer, it's important to carefully choose the type of projects you accept. Women can excel in various fields such as web design, graphic design, content writing, digital marketing, and translation while adhering to the principles of modesty and hijab. These professions can be done from home in a way that allows for personal privacy and comfort, without compromising religious duties or modesty. By choosing the right projects and maintaining a professional and modest approach, women can thrive in the freelancing world.

By ensuring that freelancing activities are conducted while upholding the values of hijab and avoiding haram work, women can build a meaningful and successful career. Freelancing allows flexibility and independence, but it also requires a strong commitment to one's faith and principles. With discipline and care, women can engage in a fulfilling freelancing career while staying true to their religious beliefs, helping them succeed both professionally and spiritually.

By integrating Islamic values into their freelancing careers, women can achieve both spiritual and professional success. Freelancing offers flexibility, independence, and the ability to earn a halal income while staying true to one's faith.

- Freelancing allows women to work from home while maintaining hijab and modesty.

- It is particularly suitable for fields like web design, content writing, graphic design, and translation.

- A safe and Islamic environment is essential for maintaining faith and modesty while working.

- Freelancing activities must align with Islamic values, avoiding any haram content or unethical projects.

- Women can successfully create and sell digital products, such as themes and templates, while earning halal income.

- Content writing and translation are ideal for women who wish to work privately and securely.

- Freelancing provides flexibility, allowing women to balance personal and professional responsibilities.

- Choosing projects carefully helps maintain Islamic integrity and professional growth.

- Upholding hijab and modesty while freelancing leads to both spiritual and career success.

- Women can thrive in freelancing by focusing on halal opportunities and aligning their work with Islamic principles.

Can You Freelance While Studying?

As a student, it's essential to recognize that focusing solely on textbooks is not always the most beneficial approach. While academics are important, it's equally crucial for a student to acquire technical skills outside of their textbooks. Reading technical books and watching video tutorials can broaden your knowledge and enhance your future career prospects. It's a common misconception that having a degree automatically guarantees a good job; however, this is often not the case. After completing your studies, you might find that creating your own opportunities and learning new skills is necessary to succeed. If you can start building these skills during your student years, it can have a significant impact on your future.

Balancing studies and freelancing can help you cover personal expenses, but it's important to note that freelancing professionally should not be the primary focus while you are still in school. Instead, your goal should be to enhance your skills and learn as much as possible in your free time. Jumping into freelancing without mastering the necessary skills can lead to poor results in both your studies and your freelance work. If you try to take on professional freelancing work before you're fully equipped with the right skills, you might find that you're unable to manage both your academic responsibilities and freelance tasks effectively.

Freelancing opens up numerous opportunities for students to enhance their skills and lay a solid groundwork for future career success:

Skill Development: Freelancing allows students to practice and refine technical skills like coding, graphic design, content writing, or digital marketing, which are valuable in the job market.

Portfolio Building: By taking on small freelance projects, students can create a portfolio that showcases their capabilities and attracts future clients or employers.

Networking: Freelancing helps students connect with professionals in their field, opening doors for mentorship, collaboration, and future job opportunities.

Earning Potential: Even with minimal experience, freelancing can provide students with a source of income to cover personal expenses or invest in further education.

Real-World Application: Freelancing projects allow students to apply theoretical knowledge from their studies to solve practical problems, enhancing their understanding and expertise.

Freelancing can be a great opportunity for students to develop essential skills, gain hands-on experience, and even earn some money in their free time. By focusing on skill development and practical experience during your student years, you can gain a significant edge when transitioning into full-time work after graduation. Freelancing allows you to apply what you learn in real-world scenarios, which can enhance your expertise and make you more competitive in the job market.

The key to balancing freelancing and studies is time management. It's important to use your time wisely and ensure that you maintain a balance between your academic responsibilities and the new skills you're learning for freelancing. By doing so, you can ensure that your studies are not neglected while also gaining valuable experience in freelancing. This balance will prepare you for future success, as you'll have both a solid academic foundation and the practical skills necessary to thrive in the workforce.

However, neglecting either your studies or skill development can harm your future prospects. If you fail to invest enough time in your education or don't properly focus on building your freelancing skills, you may find yourself unprepared for the challenges ahead. Therefore, it's essential to stay motivated, manage your time effectively, and keep learning, making the most of both your academic commitments and your freelancing opportunities.

Final Words

If you're thinking of freelancing as a way to earn endless money while doing little work from home, you might face disappointment. While there is great potential for income, it's equally true that if you don't approach freelancing the right way or fail to find work, your freelancing career could be at risk.

Start your freelancing journey only after mastering the necessary skills. Don't create a marketplace account without learning the work first. Freelancing marketplaces do not allow multiple account creations. If you fail to deliver quality work and receive negative feedback, it stays on your profile and can't be erased.

Begin by taking small jobs on the marketplace to build experience. Always strive to earn positive feedback from clients. Once you secure a job, deliver it quickly and accurately to ensure client satisfaction, which will likely lead to repeat business. Always remain honest in your work, and know that, Insha'Allah, Allah will reward you for your sincerity.

Never, under any circumstances, resort to fake reviews to get hired. Engaging in such practices can lead to your account being permanently banned. Always stay away from dishonest methods.

Work with consistency and follow a routine. Dedicate time each day to learning something new. Start your workday early after performing Fajr prayers, and avoid staying up late unless necessary. Reduce time spent on social media; you'll notice how much of your work hours can be wasted there. Instead of spending time unnecessarily hanging out with friends, use that time to learn new skills, acquire knowledge, or spend it in worship—these are the best ways to utilize your time.

Above all, never neglect your prayers due to work. Perform your prayers on time with the congregation. When the call for prayer (Adhan) sounds, pause your work and prepare for prayer; otherwise, you risk missing it. Always pray to Allah for success in your endeavors and ask Him for guidance. I also ask for your good prayers.

Keep striving to earn a halal income with all your efforts.

Insha'Allah, Allah will help you.

www.ingramcontent.com/pod-product-compliance
Lightning Source LLC
Chambersburg PA
CBHW031428210526
45464CB00005B/2102